W9-CDJ-734

03

Cover
Illustration/
Vasava

Output

Future trends 06
Spotting the styles that will
shape 2010's design

Josh Cochran 12
Meet the young creative
putting print in the mix

Designed for Life 20
Designer trinkets, gadgets
and artistic ephemera

In Depth

Icon Interview 28
tDR's Ian Anderson rises
from the flames

**Discover the hidden
power of Acrobat** 34
Unlock the true power of
Adobe's most undervalued
creative application

Profile: PetPunk 44
The Lithuanian duo
searching for the
future of design

Open Studios 50
Take a peek around some
of the most famous studios
on the planet

Technique

**Adding character
to type** 86
Tom Lane's Photoshop
typography masterclass

**Commercial
characters** 90
How to successfully mix
character and branding

**Create Flash
photo mosaics** 94
Build photo mosaic
art via your webcam

98 **Inspiration
Workshop**
Spiral Studio explains its
haunting artworks

102 **Table tips
in InDesign**
Jo Gulliver brings
simplicity to the table

103 **From Illustrator
to Flash**
Tips and tricks to move
smoothly through Flash

104 **Explosive
animation**
Alex Donne Johnson
shares his incredible
motion technique

108 **Brief Encounter**
Nick Scott Studio
celebrates Google's life

112 **Make abstract
communicate**
Gordon Reid shows you
how to clear the way in
abstract design

Need to Know

118 **Creative 3D tools**
What the latest 3d
creation techniques mean
for your work

122 **Cross media tips**
Ensure your artwork's
right for every output

Essentials

04 Contributors
22 **Opinion:** Jason Arber
24 Mail/Portfolio clinic
61 Hardware guide
116 Subscribe and save
128 Exposure
135 Next issue
137 On your CD

Creating stylised type in Photoshop _Page 86

Unlock Acrobat's power _Page 34

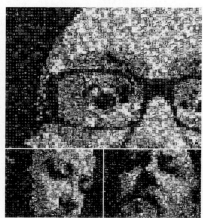

Advertising with character _Page 90

Create photo mosaics in Flash _Page 94

From this month's cover designer to some of the industry's most knowledgeable professionals, meet the people featured in this issue

Featured Creatives

Bruno Sellés
Barcelona-based design outfit Vasava can finally add a *Computer Arts* cover to its already impressive portfolio. Creative director Sellés and his team worked on this issue's intricate design.

Falko Ohlmer
The German illustrator turned around a perfect accompanying illustration to this issue's Acrobat Pro feature, examining the secrets of the app. Check out his amazing work on page 34.

Josh Cochran
Cochran's mind-bending mash-ups consist of hand-drawn illustration and print-making techniques, which combined translate to a truly unique style. Find out more on page 12.

PetPunk
Andrius Kirvela and Gediminas Šiaulys are the Lithuanian art direction and design minds behind the amazing PetPunk. We profile them and their work in our interview beginning on page 44.

Darren Hopes
Hopes is the man behind Spiral Studio, whose otherworldly mixed media art and design has graced ads for *GQ*, Sony and O2. We explore his style in this issue's Inspiration Workshop on page 98.

Tom Lane
The multi-talented hand behind Ginger Monkey returns to these pages for an expert tutorial in working with detailed type in Photoshop. Discover his techniques on page 86.

Ben Mounsey
Mounsey's commercial illustration has graced campaigns for clients including Cartoon Network and Nickelodeon. Discover how he brings character to commercial work in his superb Illustrator tutorial on page 90.

Nick Scott
Nick Scott Studio is one of the most in-demand motion and art direction houses in the UK, and its short film celebration of Google's life so far shows exactly why. Discover how it was made in Brief Encounter on page 108.

Gordon Reid
The mild-mannered man behind the fabulous Middleboop 'zine takes the reins of our second Photoshop tutorial to show you how to blend abstract elements with clear communication. Check it out on page 112.

Future Publishing Ltd, 30 Monmouth Street, Bath BA1 2BW
Phone 01225 442 244 **Fax** 01225 732 275
Email computerarts@futurenet.com
Web www.computerarts.co.uk

Editorial
Rob Carney Editor
rob.carney@futurenet.com
Tom Dennis Deputy editor
tom.dennis@futurenet.com
Jo Gulliver Art editor
jo.gulliver@futurenet.com
Luke O'Neill Deputy art editor
luke.oneill@futurenet.com
Amy Hughes Operations editor
amy.hughes@futurenet.com
Jim McCauley Online editor
jim.mccauley@futurenet.com
Jeremy Ford New media editor
jeremy.ford@futurenet.com

Contributors
Jason Arber, Graeme Aymer, Rafael Bessa, Matt Booth, Jacob Cass, Nick Carson, Alex Donne Johnson, Tim Hardwick, Tony Harmer, Falko Ohlmer, Mark Penfold, Tom Lane, Ben Mounsey, Beren Neale, Ed Ricketts, Nick Scott, Vasava, Garrick Webster, Richard Wentk, Charlotte West, Paul Wyatt

Photography Reynard Li, Joby Sessions, Jesse Wild
Cover printer Midway **Text printer** BGP
Paper Text: Graphocote 80gsm text,
Cover Precision Special Gloss 250gsm
Typeface Akkurat

Steve Jarratt Group senior editor
Robin Abbott Creative director
Christian Day Group senior art editor
Jim Douglas Editorial director

Advertising 0207 042 4122
Mark Rankine Advertising director
mark.rankine@futurenet.com
Nick Ripley Advertising manager
nick.ripley@futurenet.com
George Lucas Account sales manager
george.lucas@futurenet.com
Guy Jackson Classified sales executive
guy.jackson@futurenet.com
Malcolm Stoodley London sales director
malcolm.stoodley@futurenet.com
Jude Daniels Ad director central sales
jude.daniels@futurenet.com
Kerry Nortcliffe Ad manager central sales
kerry.nortcliffe@futurenet.com

Marketing
Daniel Bruce Brand manager
daniel.bruce@futurenet.com
Rosie Dedman Promotions executive
rosie.dedman@futurenet.com

Print & Production
Vivienne Turner Production co-ordinator
Nola Cokely Ad production manager
Richard Mason Head of production

Circulation
Laura Finnigan-Treacy
Subscriptions product manager
laura.finnigan-treacy@futurenet.com
Stuart Brown Trade marketing manager
stuart.brown@futurenet.com

Licensing
Tim Hudson International Licensing Director
tim.hudson@futurenet.com

Future Publishing Limited
Matt Pierce Group publisher
Simon Wear Chief operating officer
Robert Price Chief executive

Subscriptions
0844 848 2852
www.myfavouritemagazines.co.uk
Next issue on sale 14 January 2010

Distributed by
Seymour Distribution Ltd, 2 East Poultry Avenue, London EC1A 9PT Tel: 0207 429 4000

[**Want to work for** *Future*?
Visit www.futurenet.com/jobs]

 A member of the Audit Bureau of Circulations
21,209
Jan-Dec 2008

 Future produces carefully targeted special-interest magazines, websites and events for people who share a passion. We publish more than 170 magazines and websites and 100 international editions of our titles are published across the world.

Future plc is a public company quoted on the London Stock Exchange (symbol: FUTR).

www.futureplc.com

Chief executive Stevie Spring
Non-executive chairman Roger Parry
Group finance director John Bowman
Tel +44 (0)207 042 4000 (London)
Tel +44 (0)1225 442 244 (Bath)

FSC Mixed Sources
Product group from well-managed forests and other controlled sources
Cert no. TT-COC-1815
© 1996 Forest Stewardship Council

We are committed to only using magazine paper which is derived from well managed, certified forestry and chlorine-free manufacture. Future Publishing and its paper suppliers have been independently certified in accordance with the rules of the FSC (Forest Stewardship Council).

recycle
When you have finished with this magazine please recycle it.

RECIPES FOR SUCCESS
STARTING AT £ 0.75

housewife © olly #15997588
XL Standard / 6 Credits (£ 4.50)

SINGLE IMAGE DOWNLOAD STARTING AT £0.75 / WITHIN A SUBSCRIPTION STARTING AT 7 PENCE

Europe's No. 1 creative resource.
8 million royalty free Photos, Vectors, and Videos starting at £ 0.75.
Phone 020 881 67284 | www.fotolia.co.uk

 fotolia

Output

esign trends, the hottest illustrators and the best new work from around the world

Experience 2010

Design trends_ As the current recession hopefully abates, 2010 will be the year of designing experiences; it will be about visually engineering what your client's customers feel. This doesn't just mean massive projects like Nike Town, the Target Experience or Virgin Atlantic's total experience design, though. Small companies will also hone their customer relationships.

ContainerPLUS recently created a series of dioramas for Lutyens & Rubinstein, a new West London bookshop. The designers constructed scenes for each fiction genre – history, crime, travel, children's and science fiction. They also decorated the ceiling and, fittingly, it was all made out of books. "Like coming across a lovely book in a shop, none of the scenes aimed to shout at the viewer but simply existed to curl up amongst the shelves waiting to be found," says ContainerPLUS's Nicola Carter.

In digital, expect far greater exploration in the design of interfaces and navigation systems. 2010 is all about creating a new experience. Swiss studio Station uses a variety of inventive ways to involve visitors to their homepage: instead of pulling down menus or paging through a portfolio, you can drag elements about, flick through photos and even chase ants around the screen. "If visitors can discover something or have some sort of a revelation in the process, there will be a much stronger bond between the customer and the brand," says Patman, Station's creative director. "You don't want to browse a website, you want to experience it."

With the death of print long predicted, what does this mean for the still image? Illustrators will be looking to give their work more punch in 2010, and one answer is motion graphics. Ree Treweek, resident illustrator at South African animation company Shy the Sun, admits that her continued on page 08 →

01

In this month's Output

← **Mark Ward**
Pattern-making for the Asia launch of the new Adidas 532 range
page 9

Hugo & Marie
Introducing the creative agency's new online boutique
page 10

← **Illustrating Amelia**
Illustrators clamber to contribute to the first *Amelia's Anthology of Illustration* page 11

Bent Image Lab
Fairytale favourites are brought to life for Dr Pepper
page 11

01 A ContainerPLUS diorama for bookshop Lutyens & Rubinstein. "Graphic design, instead of being a 2D experience, can be moved into multiple dimensions where there are chances to play with sound, light, perspective, changing scales and manipulating senses," says ContainerPLUS's Nicola Carter

02 The ContainerPLUS window display for Lutyens & Rubinstein featured writing coming to life, while the interior ceiling decorations resembled books taking flight

03 Ree Treweek's work on this incredibly ornate commercial for United Airlines really caught the attention of the animation blogs last year

02

03

← **Output highlight**
Josh Cochran
He's the man pulling illustration through the printmaking grinder,

and now our Brooklyn-based one-to-watch has his sights set on a bare wall near you
page 12

← **THIS IS Studio**
Kitsch gets a moment in the awards spotlight with THIS IS Studio's trophy work page 14

Nobrow
For issue 2, the illustration publication heads to the jungle page 15 →

04 Browsing around Station's website changes the backdrop. Here a live video feed from the Station office sits behind the main interface

05 The history of Station is spelled out not just in text but in photographs that the website visitor can rearrange any way they like. It's certainly more imaginative than a timeline motif

06 A Ree Treweek work in progress. She loves designing new characters and objects that later get animated by her colleagues at Shy the Sun

→ artwork is the essence of the company's visual style, but she's not just putting her work into motion; her personal projects include sculpture, audio and even a game. "For illustrators wanting to become involved in animation, it's important to have an understanding of how the process works and how one would need to prep work for a particular animation style," Treweek advises. "But above all it's [crucial to find] a great working dynamic between yourself and other people who specialise in all the things you can't do."
www.containerplus.co.uk
www.station.ch
www.shythesun.tv

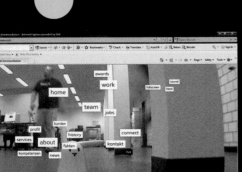

04

05

06

← **Output highlight**
The Journey
To promote the launch of its new product, Shots, Relentless has

commissioned an impressive new video work. The creative director behind it gives us a preview **page 16**

← **Ctrl. Alt. Shift**
We check out hard-hitting publication *Ctrl. Alt.Shift Unmasks Corruption* **page 17**

More design projects next month…
Issue 172 on sale
Thursday 11 February

01 Mark Ward's main panel was first used to support the Adidas 532 launch, and now hangs in Adidas Asia's Shanghai headquarters

02-03 In a follow-up commission, Adidas asked Mark Ward to create five repeating pattern prints, each inspired by one of the shoes in the collection. The patterns now decorate a display case in a high-end trainer retailer in the Far East

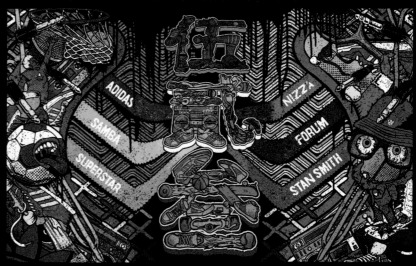

01

02

03

2010: What's in store?

Illustration
Rod Hunt,
Illustrator and Chairman of the Association of Illustrators
www.rodhunt.com

"Modern, on-demand print processes and the internet have made it easier for illustrators to create and sell their own products, including homeware, screen prints, clothing, skateboards, books, badges, art prints and more. Husband-and-wife team Fiona and Ben O'Brien (aka Ben the Illustrator) and their Wish You Were Here range shows what can be achieved."

Graphic design
Rob Brearley,
creative director, Golden
www.wearegolden.co.uk

"We've received a substantial amount of educating mailers from FSC-accredited paper mills and independent printers, which can only increase as we move into 2010. We should expect to see a rise in the use of more environmentally friendly substrates, although where that leaves our gold-foiled stationery..."

Digital
Ste Brennan, development director, Code Computerlove
www.codecomputerlove.com

"We'll see a proliferation of HTML 5-based web applications and user interfaces on both desktop and mobile browsers, especially once Google Wave begins to make a wider impact. It will be great to see even more responsive JavaScript enhanced UIs with the bedding in of faster JavaScript virtual machines such as Chrome's V8 and Firefox's TraceMonkey."

Mark Ward for Adidas

When the new Adidas 532 range – five trainers, three stripes, two garments – launched in Asia, the company hired British illustrator Mark Ward to create artwork to support the event. First up, he created the numbers five, two and three in Chinese numerals as part of an enormous wall mural for the launch in Shanghai, and he went on to create separate repeating patterns for the shoes in the collection. Inspiration came directly from the Adidas story for each trainer, covering notable sportswear influences like hip-hop, basketball and football. "It was fun to mash all these cultures together, making them fit together in the symmetrical layout I'd decided on to give a central focus on the Chinese numbers," says Ward. "My palette also helped give the work a neon sign feel that ties directly back to Shanghai."
www.markwardstudio.com
www.stemagency.com

01 An incredible scarf pattern based on the themes of love and sex was created by Benbo George for the Hugo & Marie online boutique

02 Anna Giertz's intricate pattern work is ideal for fabric products, and this scarf was created using 100 per cent eco-friendly dyes

Shopping with Hugo & Marie

New York creative agency Hugo & Marie has opened an online boutique selling a collection of products created by the talents it represents. At the boutique, punters can order silk scarves by the likes of Deanne Cheuk, Fontaine Anderson and Micah Lidberg, as well as jewellery by Marie and publications including *Newwork* magazine. "It's a way to facilitate and promote the work of people that we really love and admire," says Mario Hugo of the motivation behind the online shop. "We've been developing all kinds of scarves, lighting and jewellery with colleagues whose work we really love." The team is currently looking for small retailers worldwide to carry the range.
www.shop.hugoandmarie.com

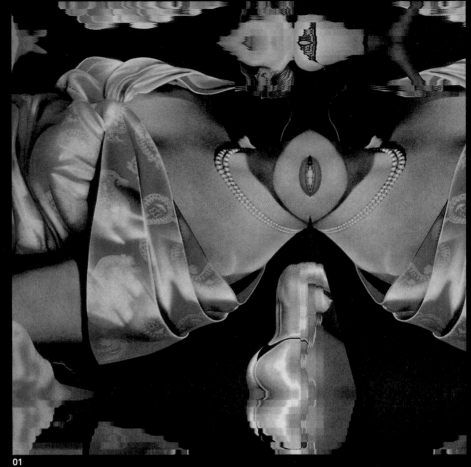

01

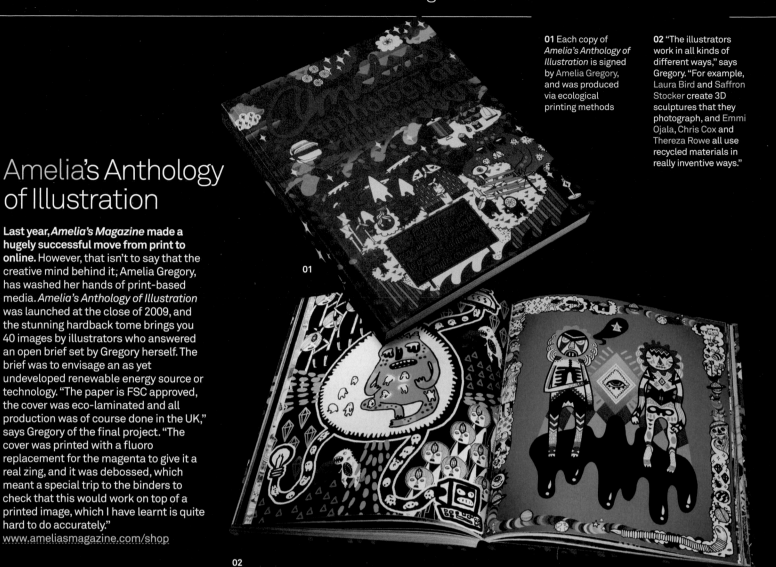

01 Each copy of *Amelia's Anthology of Illustration* is signed by Amelia Gregory, and was produced via ecological printing methods

02 "The illustrators work in all kinds of different ways," says Gregory. "For example, Laura Bird and Saffron Stocker create 3D sculptures that they photograph, and Emmi Ojala, Chris Cox and Thereza Rowe all use recycled materials in really inventive ways."

Amelia's Anthology of Illustration

Last year, *Amelia's Magazine* made a hugely successful move from print to online. However, that isn't to say that the creative mind behind it; Amelia Gregory, has washed her hands of print-based media. *Amelia's Anthology of Illustration* was launched at the close of 2009, and the stunning hardback tome brings you 40 images by illustrators who answered an open brief set by Gregory herself. The brief was to envisage an as yet undeveloped renewable energy source or technology. "The paper is FSC approved, the cover was eco-laminated and all production was of course done in the UK," says Gregory of the final project. "The cover was printed with a fluoro replacement for the magenta to give it a real zing, and it was debossed, which meant a special trip to the binders to check that this would work on top of a printed image, which I have learnt is quite hard to do accurately."
www.ameliasmagazine.com/shop

01

02

---

01 The tooth fairy shares a Diet Dr Pepper with Bigfoot. "If you're developing a character on a tight project deadline, the first thing to do is establish the style," says Bent Image Lab's Ken Lidster

02 The Bent Image Lab crew gets the performance right on set. After the stop-motion work is done, the shots are adjusted in post-production software and edited

01

02

Bent Image Lab for Dr Pepper

The latest Dr Pepper commercial produced by Bent Image Lab sounds like a dream job for anyone interested in character work. The spot focuses on what would happen if the imaginary personalities we know and love from childhood – including the Easter bunny and the tooth fairy – collectively discovered Diet Dr Pepper. Like other Bent projects, the ad was made in a stop-motion style that nestles nicely with the very current handmade aesthetic.

"How do we develop a complete character in a short commercial?" ponders director Ken Lidster. "That comes down to creating believable character nuances, and the talent of the animators. You have to take advantage of every piece of visual information the characters present: appearance, facial features and posture as well as gestures and movements."
www.bentimagelab.com

01

Josh Cochran

Meet the New York illustrator who's spearheading the drawing/printmaking mash-up scene

Josh Cochran lives in Brooklyn, New York, with his wife Jenny and their dog Pork Chop. Since graduating in 2005 from the Art Center School of Design in Pasadena, California, Cochran has been gradually building his illustration career with a style that combines the flair of a comic book artist, fantastic amounts of hand-drawn detail and colour combinations cooked up in Photoshop. His client list now includes the likes of *The New York Times*, Billabong, The Discovery Channel and Volkswagen, and in addition to the big client commissions he continues to enjoy indulging in unique personal projects.

Computer Arts: How would you characterise your style of illustration?
Josh Cochran: Drawing and printmaking mashed together.

CA: There's a clear comic book influence through your work. Which titles have inspired you?

JC: I grew up reading *The Adventures of Tintin* and the *The Adventures of Asterix*. I have always been interested in the complex, detailed worlds of Hergé. Some elements are realistic and others are quite simple and iconic.

CA: What kind of work have you been doing lately?
JC: Recently I completed a commercial for Mountain Dew with the motion company Buck. I worked closely with the creative director to design the look and keyframes of the animated spot. The process was a learning experience for me and it was really great to see my drawings expanded to different types of media.

CA: What kinds of things do you like to explore in your personal work?
JC: My personal work is really important to me as a means to explore new techniques or weird, random ideas I have floating around. I try to be pretty loose and work on projects that I wouldn't

normally have time to work on. A lot of the time, my personal pieces inform my commercial work.

CA: There seems to be a lot going on design-wise in Brooklyn at the moment. How do you find it as a creative location?
JC: There is a certain energy here in Brooklyn and New York that I haven't really felt anywhere else. My studio here at the Pencil Factory is [within] a large factory building shared by a lot of different illustrators, designers and art directors. Just being around all this talent really keeps me focused and elevates my work to new levels.

CA: Where do you hope to take your illustration career in the coming years?
JC: I'm interested in doing larger scale pieces. The Ace Hotel wallpaper I did is a great start in that direction, and I hope to do more work like that. I'm also looking forward to doing more gallery work.
www.joshcochran.net

01 Cochran's keyframes for a Mountain Dew commercial were put into motion by the animators at production company Buck

02-03 *Beautiful Decay* magazine commissioned Cochran to produce artwork for an article on the band Battles

04 Entitled 'Inside Path', this visualisation of a tiger is one of Cochran's personal works. For his canvas, he tiled pieces of vintage paper found in old books

05 One of Cochran's most memorable jobs is this cover for The Criterion Collection, which releases classic movies on DVD. For the John Huston film *Wise Blood*, Cochran was given freedom by the art director to strive for a simple, graphic solution

02

03

04

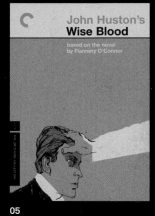

05

Starstruck Page

When designer Simon Page discovered that 2009 was the International Year of Astronomy, it caught his imagination. Independently of the organisation marking the event, IYA2009, he decided to create his own posters in tribute of it. IYA2009 ended up using them for marketing.

"My main influences were old science books and illustrations of gravitational forces and planetary motion," Page explains. "It's quite tricky to produce a design that is truly believable as a '60s or '70s design."
www.simoncpage.co.uk

Say hi to Binary & The Brain

Design duo Jawa & Midwich (AKA Simon Dovar and Nils Davey) have renamed their partnership Binary & The Brain. The original name, says Simon Dovar, was just a placeholder that stuck when the duo set up: "As Binary & The Brain was floated it just clicked for us both. It's a perfect metaphor for the way we work and the work we produce."
www.binaryandthebrain.com

Skating babies scoop awards

The Guinness Book of Records **has started counting downloads,** and has declared Evian's roller-skating babies video to be the most viewed viral ad of all time with well over 45 million downloads. The work is the result of director Michael Gracey, with visual effects trickery by the Moving Picture Company for agency BETC Euro RSCG. It also won the Best Visual Effects award at last year's London Animation Festival.
www.moving-picture.com

01 A selection of THIS IS Studio's ECCA awards package work. The making of the trophies themselves became part of the design theme of the entire project

02 Each award has its own accompanying leaflet. THIS IS Studio's trophies were also the focus of the visual message in each competition category

03 At first, THIS IS worked with velvet backdrops and confetti, but later decided the trophies were already quite kitsch enough!

01

02

03

THIS IS Studio kitsch trophies

When THIS IS Studio was asked to create an awards package for the Enterprise Centre for the Creative Arts (ECCA) late last year, the team discovered that it pays to be cautious with kitsch. The ECCA brief included trophies for design, fashion and art, as well as posters, a booklet, leaflets, bags and a web banner. THIS IS decided to create the trophies by hand first, then let the rest of the identity take its cue from them. They shot the trophies against velvet backgrounds and confetti. "It wasn't until we started laying the images up that we realised they looked a surreal mix between soft porn and beauty pageant," laughs THIS IS co-founder Barney Beech. "After that moment of clarity, the only option was to re-shoot at our own expense. The final aesthetic was much more pared back, using plain white backgrounds."
www.thisisstudio.co.uk

Design Showcase

01 French illustrator Blexbolex created the cover of issue 2 of *Nobrow*, of which a limited run of only 3000 copies are available

02 Up-and-coming illustrator Eda Akaltun's response to *Nobrow* issue 2's jungle theme. With pages of 240mmx340mm, the artists have a large area with which to get creative

01

02

Nobrow: The Jungle

Celebrating illustration and quality printing, the second issue of *Nobrow* is out now. With a jungle theme, it is priced at £15 and includes work from the likes of Marc Boutavant, Pietari Posti and Eda Akaltun, and a cover by Blexbolex. "Nobrow Press is all about publishing beautifully tactile illustrated books," says co-founder Alex Spiro. "Wherever possible we try to push the printing process to ensure that colour, format and paper quality combine to produce publications that are not just books but collectible art objects. I was very impressed by Mark Hearld's submission, which arrived in an oversized envelope with the separations all crafted by hand on layout paper. That really embodies what we are about, combining the traditional processes with the latest developments in printing technology."
www.nobrow.net

www.computerarts.co.uk

0845 017 1015
WWW.QANTM.CO.UK

Scholarships available at: mycreativefuture.com

Fast track your career in Games, Web or Animation

Accredited DEGREES* & DIPLOMA
* Validated by Middlesex University

Next Open Day 2010: Sun 21st February

01 The intensity of *The Journey* is captured in the Relentless Shot. In this cut, even the tattoos on the arms are animated

02 *The Journey* takes viewers on a conceptual trip backwards through worlds within worlds, past organic, chemical and molecular-inspired imagery

01

The Journey

With the launch of its new product, Shots, the Relentless company commissioned a piece of video that would convey the power and intensity of the drink. Ross Cairns, creative director at branding agency Erasmus, worked with Smoke & Mirrors to produce *The Journey*.

Computer Arts: What was the overall visual feel you were aiming for with *The Journey*?
Ross Cairns: The creative idea behind the ad is that 'There's more to this little bottle than meets the eye'. The narrative expression of it is a fantastic journey through worlds within worlds. This is, of course, a metaphor for the compression of a vast amount of energy into one intense hit.

CA: How did you ensure the film integrated with the overall brand message for Relentless?
RC: Relentless is inherently a dark brand, but never gratuitously. We built it on a simple truth – that you only get what you put in – so from the beginning it has been wrapped up in the visual lexicon of sacrifice and suffering. With this spot we had an additional challenge, which was to evoke raw power from something very small indeed: the product.

CA: What was the inspiration behind the imagery in the film?
RC: We wanted to evoke power and use the 'modern baroque' visual language that we have created in all Relentless branding and communications. The cellular journey idea came from the concept that when the product is consumed, some kind of atomic or molecular process will begin that you won't be able to contain.

02

CA: Apart from the very start of the spot, the camera movement is nearly all pull-back. How did you approach the animation and pacing?
RC: The feeling of calm at the beginning was very deliberate – almost like the calm before the storm – but then all hell breaks loose and there's no stopping it. Pace was always going to play an important a part in the spot. And the sound design really helps to involve the viewer.

CA: What was the biggest challenge in creating this spot?
RC: Getting the right tone, definitely. That affected everything from the idea to the technical side of things. It all had to add up and strike the right note in terms of raw, bristling power.

www.erasmuspartners.com
www.smoke-mirrors.com
www.relentlessenergy.com/pages/energyshot

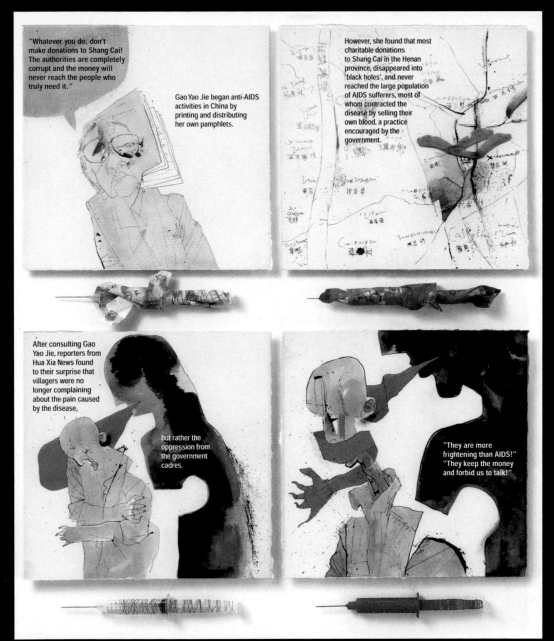

"Whatever you do, don't make donations to Shang Cai! The authorities are completely corrupt and the money will never reach the people who truly need it."

Gao Yao Jie began anti-AIDS activities in China by printing and distributing her own pamphlets.

However, she found that most charitable donations to Shang Cai in the Henan province, disappeared into 'black holes', and never reached the large population of AIDS sufferers, most of whom contracted the disease by selling their own blood, a practice encouraged by the government.

After consulting Gao Yao Jie, reporters from Hua Xia News found to their surprise that villagers were no longer complaining about the pain caused by the disease,

but rather the oppression from the government cadres.

"They are more frightening than AIDS!" "They keep the money and forbid us to talk!"

01

01 Tactile to the point of being scary, Dave McKean's comic strip asks where money donated to help AIDS victims in China actually goes

02-03 *Ctrl.Alt.Shift Unmasks Corruption*: the gallery show and graphic novel that aim to expose corrupt practices across the world

Ctrl.Alt.Shift Unmasks Corruption

Ctrl.Alt.Shift last month made a political statement using comic art and an exhibition at the Lazarides Gallery in London, entitled *Ctrl.Alt.Shift Unmasks Corruption*. Dave McKean, Pat Mills, Peter Kuper, Dan Goldman and many other top names were commissioned to create two to six-page strips. Their work focussed on corruption around the world, from US college campuses to the Congo. For Ctrl. Alt.Shift director Katrin Owusu, collaborations like that between 2004 UNICEF Photographer of the Year Marcus Bleasdale and illustrator Paul O'Connell made for powerful work. "Paul O'Connell worked with Marcus's original pictures of the Congo and created a really dramatic comic strip from them," Owusu explains. "It's very intense; full of stark red and black imagery."

In addition to the exhibition, a limited run, 100-page graphic novel containing all the exhibited illustrations is available for just £4.99.
www.ctrlaltshift.co.uk

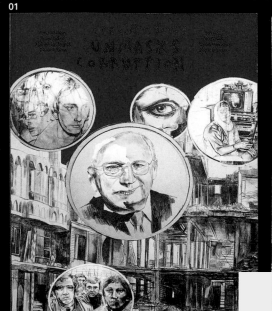

02

03

New books
Our monthly round-up of the best new design tomes to pile on your studio shelves

01 Art for Obama
Editor: Shepard Fairey and Jennifer Gross/**Publisher:** Abrams Image
ISBN: 9780810984981/**Price:** £14.99
Ranging from aerosol murals to Etch A Sketch imagery, this collection of 150 pieces of art inspired by the political rise of Barack Obama is threaded by a giddy admiration for the 44th president. At times the one-dimensional hero-worshipping recalls the partisan propaganda of more sinister political figureheads, which isn't helped by the specifics of Obama's politics being largely overlooked. But there's no denying the emotive power of the artwork, which makes this an absorbing account of how art can create and sell icons.

02 Ark: The Ark Project
Author: DGPH/**Publisher:** Systems Design Ltd/**ISBN:** 9789881847010
Price: £22
Linked to the art studio DGPH's fundraising Ark Project, this is a book with heart-on-sleeve good intentions. DGPH artists Martin Lowenstein, Diego Vaisberg and Andres Vaisberg have got over 200 artists from around the world to depict their favourite animals or species, with profits from the book and subsequent exhibitions going to wildlife charities. What's most impressive, though, is the sustained high quality of art that matches the diversity of the subject matter, starting with a take on the biblical story of Noah.

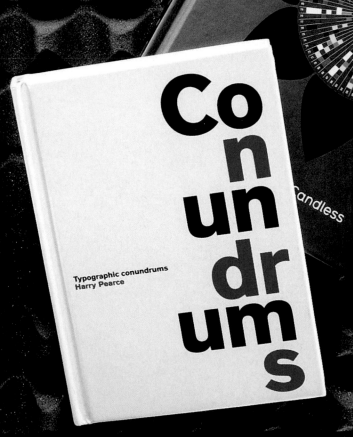

03 Conundrums

Author: Harry Pearce/**Publisher:** Harper Collins/**ISBN:** 9780061826597
Price: £9.99

_____ Although in his intro author Harry Pearce cites irreverent tricksters like Spike Milligan and Peter Cook as inspiration for his visual wordplays, there's more to this book than nutty puns. Amongst the 171 typographical conundrums within, Pearce masterfully displays the power of restraint, with each limited to one box, two colours and a single, simple typeface (AG Old Face). And with phrases like 'half cut' and 'six feet under' to decipher, the inspired use of typography is nearly always in sync with the author's humour.

04 Information is Beautiful

Author: David McCandless/**Publisher:** Harper Collins/**ISBN:** 9780007294664
Price: £20

_____ Sold as a visual journey through 'the most revealing trends and vital statistics of the modern world,' this book is actually an eclectic mix of quirky facts conveyed via a breathtaking range of design styles. David McCandless is interested in enjoying information for the fun of it, but that's only half the story. There is memorable design here, and whether you're looking at international salad dressing ingredients or potential causes of cancer, it's the author's beautifully balanced artwork that will make the biggest impression.

05 Designers Against Tibetan Abuse

Editor: Rishi Sodha/**Publisher:** Designers Against Human Rights Abuse
ISBN: To be confirmed/**Price:** £12

_____ With 52 artists involved, this collection of pro-independent Tibet design offers a mixed bag. A seeming contradiction to the uniformed cover that suggests order and clarity, the design work inside the book touches on the politically sound, earnestly ethical and, in one case, plain daft. Artists like Christopher Cox and Oliver Wiegner offer honest, heartfelt sentiment on the importance of action in aiding Tibetans from China's systematic suppression. These are just some of the many gems of politically fuelled design here.

Designed for Life
All the coolest products, gadgets and toys on sale this month

DesignByThem
jewellery tree

Produced by designers Sarah Gibson and
Nicholas Karlovasitis, the Treeling is a jewellery
storage idea inspired by the Japanese bonsai.
With branches to hang all your finest rocks and
pendants on, it's a neat design solution cut from
powder-coated mild steel sheets.
$70AUD
www.designbythem.com

Beauchampet
rings

Dutch designer Zelda Beauchampet produces
quirky and quaint items like these Handscape
rings. Each ring in the pack of three carries a
landscape element, so you can arrange your
hand-landscape (see what they've done there)
according to your mood.
€85
www.zlda.nl

Paul Smith
gadget protection

Keep your gadgets scratch-free in style with Paul Smith's latest
collection, including a classic Mini Cooper laptop sleeve, and
pinstripe iPhone cases and iPod sleeves.
From £30
www.paulsmith.co.uk

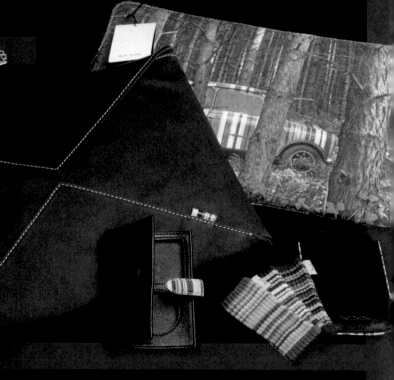

Ibruegger mugs

Need a quick disguise? Grab a moustache mug from designer Peter Ibruegger in any one of six splendid forms, including Fu-Magnum, Mustafa-Chaplin and the classic Maurice-Poirot.
£11.95
www.peteribruegger.com

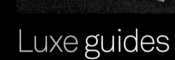

Luxe guides

It's all in the name, really, for Luxe City Guides – the most comprehensive and beautifully manufactured pocket guidebooks on the market. Each volume is distilled from the recommendations of people who actually live in each city, and collated by a resident editor into a slimline, design-conscious volume.
£4.99 each
www.luxecityguides.com

Mondaine wristwatch

Mondaine has been producing the official timepiece of the Swiss Railways since 1986, and this classic model has just been released in all its classic Swiss design glory.
£129.99
www.mondaine.com

Alkr urban protection laptop sleeve

These fine neoprene sleeves are just the job for protecting your mobile pride and joy, featuring a cushioned interior with soft fleece lining and a sleek, minimalist style care of designer Philippe Intraligi.
€30
www.alkr.com

Opinion
Jason Arber

Jason Arber
—A co-founder of Wyld Stallyons, an animation and motion graphics company based in London, Jason has worked for clients including MTV and ITV. Currently, Jason is patiently explaining to a client that "louder... but also quieter" is not, in any realistic sense, constructive feedback. To find out more visit www.wyldstallyons.com

My mum has some good logo ideas...

Clients say the funniest things. But they pay the bills, so **Jason Arber**'s not laughing

There's no getting away from it: clients can be idiotic beyond belief. Their stupidity knows no bounds. My good friend and Wyld Stallyons co-founder Chris Sayer likes to tell a story from his previous company about filming some actors in front of a green screen that was to be keyed out and replaced by jungle foliage. When the rushes were presented to the client for approval, he freaked out. "Is this your idea of a jungle?" he spluttered, jabbing a finger at the raw, un-keyed green screen footage. Once a mild sedative had been applied, it was gently explained that a more, ahem, *realistic* jungle would be inserted once the shot was in post-production.

We all have similar tales we can tell. A friend on Twitter relayed the following gem concerning a character he was animating: the client asked, "Can we close the character's eyes to show he's not listening?" Certainly. And perhaps we could close his mouth to show that he's no longer watching...?

Another friend (sorry to be so vague, but I promised to keep the identities secret) recalled a recent conversation with a client who was telling him how quickly an edit needed to be done. The client blurted out, "Look, I only work at the BBC, I don't know how editing works. Can't we just get the 10 hours of footage into two minutes this afternoon?" The mind boggles. If people at the BBC don't know how editing works, what hope do any of us have?

My favourite kind of comment tends to be the one where a client has sought a second opinion on a design, usually canvassing their mum, the milkman or even the cat. Within the last couple of weeks I was earnestly told by a client that they'd run a design I'd created past Sandra in accounts, who said the design made her feel "sad". Curiously, I'd asked the opinion of a courier who was collecting a parcel bound for Leeds, and who stated that the design made him feel "happy". We were now at something of an impasse...

I was reminded of these sorry stories by Matthew Inman's comic strip at *The Oatmeal*, called 'How a Web Design goes Straight to Hell'. It details how a website design starts off great but quickly goes off the rails once the client starts getting 'creative'. In the strip, the client says, "So this design is perfect, but I'm the CEO so I feel obligated to make changes to feel like I've done my job properly. Also, I'll use phrases like 'user experience' and 'conversion orientated' to sound smart even though I barely know how to use a computer..."

If that seems familiar, then you're going to love clientsfromhell.tumblr.com, which is full of anonymously submitted tales of client ineptitude and imbecility, such as this pearl of client wisdom: "I want this site to be really beautiful; a truly iconic web design. Something like Google, YouTube or MySpace." Or how about this: a client's response to the first draft of an eight-page brochure containing Lorem Ipsum placeholder text: "I don't think we should put the text in French. It might seem a bit elitist to people who can't read it. Otherwise, it all looks fine..."

Of course, not every client was dropped on their head as a baby. You should cherish those clients who make intelligent and informed comments, because, frankly, they're in short supply. Now if only I can figure out a way to run a business without having to deal with clients at all...

What can you do with a website?

Well, a whole host of things actually.

So take some notes...

OPEN AN E-SHOP   PUBLISH A BLOG   GET FREE APPS   SAVE ON DOMAINS

SECURE YOUR DATA   INSTALL DATABASES   GET UK SUPPORT   UPLOAD MEDIA

 Everything is made easy with 123-reg. Whatever you want to do online, we'll have it sorted in minutes.

GET STARTED NOW!
CALL US ON 0845 859 0018

Use this voucher code to get an
extra 5% off hosting: Arts04A01

Mail

computerarts@futurenet.com

Cover versions and tutorial requests– deputy art editor Luke O'Neill replies to your queries

Luke O'Neill
—This month deputy art editor Luke has mainly been posting to Ffffound.com and living a clean, healthy and balanced lifestyle, having banished the demons of Christmas for yet another year.

Did our Serial Cut cover whet your Cinema 4D appetite? See page 104 for more

Twitter feed

Who's talking about us on Twitter and what they're saying. Follow us at http://twitter.com/computerarts

@computerarts loving the Light Painting tutorial guys! Note that to get the .fla to work, you need to change export to Adobe AIR, not Flash :)
@glidepro

@ComputerArts Just received your new issue in the office! Very sexy cover! Not just the model you've used!
@acampion

@ComputerArts New mag has just landed. Loving the front cover illustration by Serial Cut. Better get the kettle on!
@TheWhiteBalance

Massive Props To @Tan_One And @Jimicrayon for the feature in @computerarts! 2010 really will be a big year for you guys!
@AlanHarford

Going digital

I must say how much I enjoy your magazine. I found several other magazines that were devoted exclusively to Photoshop but not the other Creative Suite programs. I'm an illustrator and artist and was working on paper, boards and canvas before switching to computers in 2002. I've been working in this career since I was 18. I'm now 74.

Your magazine is refreshing in that it gives projects in all the Creative Suite programs, and keeps updating to the latest versions. The only negative observation I have about your magazine is that the covers – though very different – have the same graphic shapes and lines, as if all the designers had the same lecturer and just put their own spin on it. None seem to have a story to them!
Jim Gully

Hi Jim, thanks for the email, and glad to hear that we have a reader with such an extensive design history.

Cover wise, we carefully select artists and designers who we feel are producing the most exciting new work around. The balance is between trend-hitting, impactful work and what we see as a solid cover image. Our cover artists and designers all work from the tight briefs we set them, but bring their individuality to the piece in the detail. Who do you think would make a great cover artist? Do let us know via the Computer Arts forum, Twitter or the email address at the top of the page.

Cover lover

I absolutely loved the cover Serial Cut produced for issue 170 – what a brilliant mix of style and technique! I also really enjoyed the 'making of' article in the mag by the guys at the studio.

What I'd really like to see, though, is a tutorial on this 3D montage technique, showing me step-by-step how to create that look. Any chance?
David Llewellyn

Hi David, glad you liked it. If anything reinforces our cover artist policy it's letters like yours, and we were certainly blown away with the results when Serial Cut delivered the cover artwork.

While we don't have that exact technique covered, we do have a fantastic Cinema 4D tutorial in this very issue by the super talented Alex Donne Johnson, which you can check out on page 104. What's more, Alex will be showing you how to bring these types of creations to life in the second part of his tutorial next issue – so don't miss it!

Have pen, will work

How do I get to do a tutorial for your magazine? I've been working on some amazing projects for some super-name clients, and think some of the stuff I do would make a great article.
JS, via email

Well JS, I admire your resolve, and if you send us some work we'll certainly take a look. We pride ourselves on serving up new, exciting and working tutorials written by creative professionals. This means that our tutorials highlight new techniques, new trends, exciting advancements and industry secrets from the professionals. So, if you have any specific ideas for a new and interesting techniques or tutorials, or you spot a designer whose style you'd love to see in the mag, let us know – we're always on the look out for the most interesting and skillful work out there.

Contact Computer Arts
Have you got something to say about this magazine or the design industry in general? If so, please send your comments to **30 Monmouth Street, Bath BA1 2BW** or email them to computerarts@futurenet.com

01 Exploring new techniques will further broaden illustrator **Spiros Halaris**'s professional horizons

02 Joshua Lim's strong work shows a useful versatility. All he needs now is a website to do it justice…

03 By focussing more on his core illustration skills, **Steve Cardo** will showcase his true skills to potential clients

Portfolio clinic

computerarts@futurenet.com

Art editor Jo Gulliver and deputy art editor Luke O'Neill cast their eyes over your portfolios

I'm an illustrator who's been inspired by your magazine and I would love to hear your feedback on my portfolio. I am looking forward to your comments and I would be honoured to feature.
Spiros Halaris
www.behance.net/andy505

Jo says: Hi Spiros, you're clearly a solid illustrator who can turn your hand to varied and interesting fashion work. I do feel, though, that your style is rather one-dimensional, so perhaps exploring new techniques and scenarios might lead to more work.

Luke says: I like your use of texture and hand-drawn elements, Spiros, and your restricted colour palette and economy of line makes for very stylised work. Some of your earlier pieces are a little crude in comparison to your recent work, and you may find it difficult breaking into fashion illustration, but by broadening your style you could well make your own opportunities.

I just got my portfolio done up. Would love to know your comments, find out where I stand and grow from it. Hope to hear from you guys soon!
Joshua Lim
www.edgeworks.sg

Jo says: Thanks for the email, Joshua. You have a broad portfolio of design work that shows the wide array of styles you're comfortable with. Unfortunately this is all hidden behind a rather frustrating website. Get yourself a

simple WordPress blog or similar, and post your work to there where potential clients can view it in all its glory.

Luke says: I agree with Jo here, Joshua: good, solid and slick design work with a heavy commercial leaning, but the annoying site navigation and small images dampen the effect. However, there's a broad range of commercial applications for work like this, so think a bit more about self-promotion and not just your core design work.

As a subscriber and avid reader of Computer Arts, I'd love to know what you guys think of my newly launched site. Thanks a lot!
Steve Cardno
www.stevecardno.co.uk

Jo says: Hi Steve, thanks for reading and glad to see the magazine's spurred you on creatively. You obviously have a solid understanding of Photoshop and its many effects and filters, but it would be worthwhile stripping back on the gloss and focusing in on your core illustration.

Luke says: I think you show a great sense of narrative, Steve, and clearly know your way around creative applications. Again, though, there seems to be an over-reliance on filters and effects as opposed to composition and clarity. Why not concentrate on developing the illustration side of your work so that you're able to show potential clients the real skills you possess?

01

edgeworks

Saatchi LAB

It is a great privilege to have worked with Saatchi LAB, better known as Saatchi & Saatchi. Our task here was to animate the graphics and develop a Flash application which includes an information site in four languages, a mini game, and a customisable greeting card builder.

02

03

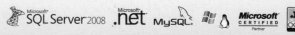

Ian Anderson

— A product of the punk era with a proudly subversive streak, Ian Anderson is the idiosyncratic founder of tDR, the Sheffield-based creative powerhouse that he spearheaded from 1986 to 2009. With an open disregard for meaningless eye-candy and a refusal to compromise ("the opposite of 'good' isn't 'bad', it's 'ok' in neatly-pressed slacks")

Anderson's design philosophy dictates that visual communication should have integrity and a solid idea at its core. Having graced the halls of global super-brands from Nokia to Coca-Cola, Sony to Nickelodeon, his pioneering work has countless imitators but few equals. He is currently creative director of EXD, the Lisbon Biennale. **www.thedesigners republic.com**

Ian Anderson

"tDR's default starting position was that the client's always wrong. I apologise. It was the fucking account executives all along." The Designers Republic founder talks punk ideologies with **Nick Carson**

Design Icons
Ian Anderson

01 Viva la Republica:
Powerful creative
autonomy remains a
guiding principle in Ian
Anderson's work,
whether that's in the
role of Lisbon Biennale's
creative director or the
design brains behind
Jarvis Cocker's album
cover artwork

01

As with so many iconic design outfits, The Designers Republic had its early roots in the music industry. Founded to create flyers, it grew organically into one of the world's most influential creative studios, famed for its defiant disregard for the design establishment, its subversive sloganeering and its trend-busting dedication to putting creativity before all else. Compare tDR to Andy Warhol's Factory, and its opinionated founder Ian Anderson would unquestionably be Warhol. A year after he closed his office doors for the last time and struck out alone, Anderson shares the uncompromising approach that's inspired a generation of designers from São Paulo to Sarajevo.

Computer Arts: It's been said that you ran tDR like a record label, with conceptual ideas and freeform creativity taking centre stage. How would you describe your design process?
Ian Anderson: To me, 'freeform creativity' suggests creativity without direction. More accurate is a commitment to creating freedom for creativity to grow, rather than to the letter of a brief. I forgot that for a while, and went bust. Creativity is not born of consensus: I think in terms of solving puzzles, and making connections. I don't trust anyone who claims they're just providing a service for the client – good creatives do it for themselves, and the client benefits from that amplified input.

CA: Did managing a band [Person to Person] give you a fresh perspective when you first founded tDR?

IA: There was a seamless evolution from managing bands to designing for them. The beauty of being the band's designer, rather than their manager, was that I got to create the shit rather than having to clear it up.

I guess it's unavoidable that I had a different perspective. My natural tendency is to use words, colour and form to express my thinking. Graphic design, in the current vernacular, holds little appeal for me. Designers who are essentially graphic stylists are an enigma – what a fucking waste of time. That's all the more ironic given that, for significant periods of tDR's history, our visual styling was so copied that people forgot there was an idea behind it in the first place.

CA: Your work for Warp Records brought tDR to a bigger stage. Would you draw parallels between the Warp/tDR relationship in Sheffield and Saville/Factory in Manchester? Do you see iconic music designers such as Saville, Brody and Garrett as influential forerunners?
IA: You could draw parallels, but I wouldn't; neither would I regard Neville, Peter and Malcolm as iconic, or anything other than passionate and eloquent fellow designers, although undeniably some of their work has proved to be iconic over the years.

tDR kicked against the 'establishment' attitude – a non-sensibility fattened on the loadsamoney dollar, patting itself on the back for running ideas up the flagpole to see who saluted them. There were people who personified all that, but we weren't interested in them. With an increasingly

distant past, it tends to be the effects, not the causes, which are remembered.

CA: Did your sloganeering, anti-consumerist attitude stem from the original punk movement. Are those your musical roots?
IA: The original UK punk revolution, the first cultural year zero since the birth of teenagers, happened to kick off when I was ripe for being influenced. Living with a trade unionist father during the dark socio-political days of the three-day-week '70s, punk wasn't a spectator sport.

Like graphic design for me now, the music then was an expression for something I perceived to be much bigger. Punk only lasted for six months prior to it going overground, but its cultural resonance is still felt now because it was an idea, not just three chords. That might be why way too many flyers these days look like they fell out of tDR's bins in the '90s.

CA: When expanding the studio, did you deliberately seek out designers who shared your wider philosophy and approach?
IA: We always called it the 'office'. Everyone I knew with a 'studio' was a musician or an artist. It grew organically as it needed to – if you choose the right people to work with, it makes sense to give them creative freedom, so they deliver according to their ego, not your expectations. Clients should understand this too: it's more cost effective than sitting through numerous pitches where creatives are basically second-guessing what they want. →

The essential DR

01 Warp Records logo

02 WipEout packaging

03 Emigre magazine

02 Steely reserve:
Anderson's continued efforts to kick against "culturally fly-tipping" remain rooted in tDR's home city of Sheffield

02

→ I tried to identify fellow travellers, people with something to learn, something to prove, something to say. [Latterly], I made a big mistake employing people to satisfy particular types of client. That doesn't work if you want creativity at the core rather than business – it was a step towards satisfying, rather than exceeding, clients' expectations.

CA: Your early work has clear Soviet influences, which permeate the language of the studio – The Republic, The Peoples Bureau, and so on. How have politics influenced your approach to design?
IA: I see politics as something to opt out of, not something you choose to get involved in. As designers, our work is public, so we have a responsibility to enhance the environment – otherwise we're just culturally fly tipping.
I'm interested in big messages, in absolutes. Revolutionary art and propaganda is always extremely potent, because of the verve and passion of the progenitors, coupled with the willingness of the adherents to comply. I'm interested in the similarities between huge roadside billboards in Communist states – urging the people on to greater productivity – and the consumerist subtexts inherent in every billboard hoarding everywhere.

CA: tDR's critics have drawn attention to your heavily kerned, heavily designed and at times unreadable typography. How do you respond?
IA: Fuck 'em, and damn their pissy little rules. Words are expressive; language should be bent out of shape. How else can we express new ideas in a torpid, static language that's evolved to explain old ones?
In the late '80s we tried to develop a 'universal global visual slang' based on modern Japanese type-based designs. We couldn't read Japanese, but we could understand them because of the multinational corporate logos that populated the work. Understanding the sense of something – the spirit of it – is more important than legibility.

CA: In recent years, did having a relatively large studio to sustain pull you into a vicious circle where smaller, cooler projects just weren't practical?

IA: I think the fact that the successful work I did for Coca-Cola worked across every cultural and linguistic mix on the planet is cooler than selling a limited number of cracking or storming 12"s out of the back of a van. But that's just me.
Unfortunately, the type of person who wants to deliver forward-thinking design doesn't always sit well with the type of person who feeds the larger corporate clients. They build relationships based on business compatibility, not the ability to deliver great visual communication – as opposed to budget-busting eye candy. tDR's default starting position was that the client's always wrong. I apologise. It was the fucking account executives all along.
I don't regret taking on high-profile projects; I regret employing people purely to feed those projects on the clients' terms, rather than ours. A large studio wasn't sustainable because there wasn't an internal fit. You can lead horses to water, but you can't make them drink. It's better now. For everyone.

CA: Do you feel a greater sense of creative freedom now that you've scaled everything back to the core? How do you operate now?
IA: The future is communication by any means necessary. I'm working on collaborations, as a consultant and with tDR. I'm going to spend some time being Ian Anderson, and see who wants a slice of that. I want to do more than the designer superstar straightjacket allowed.
I'd like to see what it's like working with people who were considered devils incarnate by tDR, just to see what happens. There are tDR books, and there's a mighty retrospective tDR festival coming up in Tokyo in 2011. There's plenty to do but, unsurprisingly, having an oversized studio hanging round my neck isn't one of them. I'm using other people's studios from now on.

Language should be bent out of shape. How else can we express new ideas in a torpid, static language that's evolved to explain old ones?

F8 AT 30 WEEKS

Zena Holloway
Underwater Photographer

Shot by Nick Simpson
Equipment supplied by Zena, OMD & Kinetic

BIRMINGHAM NEC 7–10 MARCH 2010

Trade registration: 01489 882 800 | Online registration: www.focus-on-imaging.co.uk
Non trade you're welcome! Only £10 on site (£8 if pre-paid on-line)

FOCUS
on imaging
SHARE THE PASSION

Tel: 020 8681 2619 • Fax: 020 8667 1590 • Email: info@focus-on-imaging.co.uk • Image House, Coombe Avenue, Croydon CR0 5SD UK

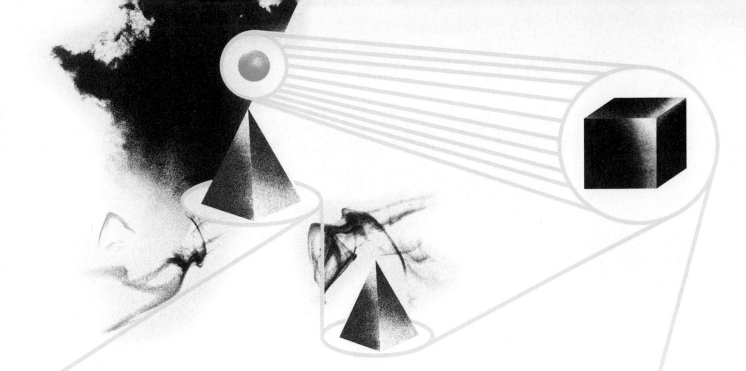

The power of Acrobat

Adobe Acrobat Pro is an underrated piece of kit. When partnered with Adobe's Creative Suite programs, it can transform the way you work and deliver that work. All that's required from you is a certain amount of Acrobat know-how…

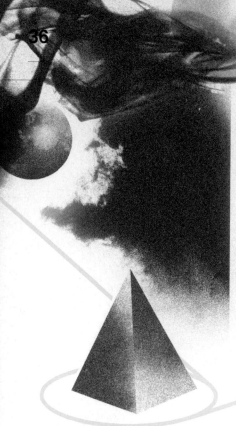

Acrobat 9 Pro: Your interactive tool

Discover how to tap into Acrobat's interactive side to enhance your PDFs and give your work a dynamic edge

We all have an unfortunate habit of taking Acrobat Pro for granted. And why wouldn't we? It's so reliable when you need to view, create, mark up and exchange files in the PDF format. In fact, it's such a dependable, seamless tool that you sometimes fail to notice all the help it has given you. But there's so much more you could be doing with it...

Acrobat Pro can help you impress clients, streamline your workflow and add the 'wow' factor that's lacking in standard PDF presentations and folios. It's just a matter of knowing the tools and buttons that turn Acrobat Pro into a seriously great piece of kit, one that is both creative and interactive. Acrobat 9 Pro has bolstered its feature list to include greater output preview and pre-flight enhancements, which are

Photoshop and InDesign CS4, Acrobat 9 Pro

Build an interactive portfolio in Acrobat 9 Pro

Paul Wyatt demonstrates just how simple it is to present your work interactively with a little help from Acrobat

Paul Wyatt
___ Paul Wyatt has created websites, animation work and broadcast creative for clients such as Talkback Thames, D&AD, Virgin Media and the BBC. To find out more, visit www. paulwyatt.co.uk

On the disc
The files relating to this tutorial can be located in DiscContents\ Resources\Acrobat

Time needed
1-2 hours

Skills
___ Working between InDesign and Acrobat
___ Portfolio layout
___ Set up interactive button properties

01_____ From this issue's disc, open the file navigation_images.psd. This element will serve as our main menu device, which we'll optimise and then add interactivity to in Acrobat 9 Pro. Turn the background layer visibility off, then select File>Save for Web & Devices. Save as Preset: PNG-24, and check the Transparency box. Name this file navigation_images.png.

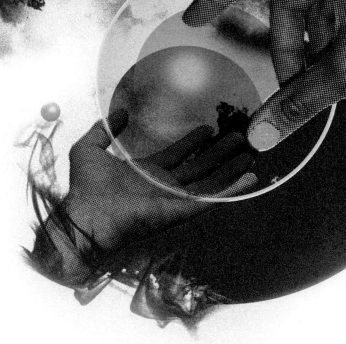

absolutely essential when it's your job to make sure there are no problems with the files you send to press. You can now perform checks and fix-ups on selected objects, as well as being able to validate PDF/E compliance and saving documents in PDF/E format. There's also a number of colour conversion enhancements in 9 Pro, enabling you to remap spot colours via the Pantone library, convert colours and set a transparency blending space.

If you're an agency who sends out credential presentations to potential clients, you can now bank brownie points by surprising them with a presentation containing webpage-style links, rollovers and forms. Take it a step further and include Flash videos and animations with Acrobat

Pro's native support for Flash. If you want to completely knock their socks off, you could include an interactive PDF map for your presentation, one that uses geo-spacial data enabling you to view location co-ordinates and measure distances.

And it doesn't end there. We've compiled a list of the lesser-known but hugely valuable Acrobat Pro functions, and in the following pages you'll also find a tutorial to help you get to grips with implementing these functions into your workflow. We'll show you how to make a folio/credentials presentation which functions like a webpage, complete with interactive links, rollovers and an email form. Your relationship with Acrobat Pro is about to enter an exciting new phase... →

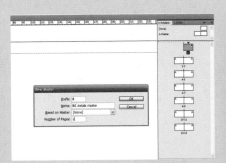

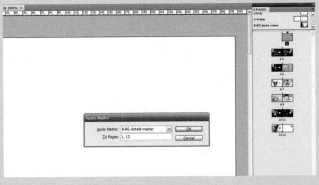

02_____ Open folio_partial.indd in InDesign. We'll need to create a master page containing the background elements for the navigation and contact pages. Select Window>Pages. In the Pages panel, select 'New master' then, in the pop-up options box, enter the name 'BG details master'. Change the number of pages to 1.

03_____ Double-click the 'BG details master' page to edit it. Select File>Place, navigate to the file 'BG_element.jpg' then double-click it. Now click in the top right-hand corner of the master page to place the image. Select Window>Layers and click in the blank box next to the eye icon to lock this layer.

04_____ Return to the Pages panel and double-click the small page preview icon for Page 1. Right-click on this page and select 'Apply master to pages'. In the Apply Master menu of the dialog box, select 'B-BG details master' and in the To Pages box type '1, 13'. The background for each slide will now change.

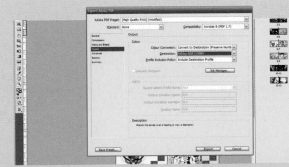

05_____ Select File>Place and place the image navigation_images.png to the left of Page 1, as shown in the screenshot. Select File>Export. Save the file as interactive_folio.pdf. In the Export Adobe PDF options box, select Output from the left-hand menu and change the Colour Destination setting to 'Adobe RBG (1998)'. Hit the Export button.

06_____ Open interactive_folio.pdf in Adobe Acrobat 9. Select Tools>Advanced Editing>Show Advanced Editing Toolbar. Create an interactive push button by clicking the Button tool. Click and drag out a grey square which covers the first menu item image on the first page. When prompted, give this the label name 'Menu item 1'.

07_____ Double-click the grey square to reveal the Button Properties panel. Select the Appearance tab and click the 'Fill color' colour picker. Select 'No color', then the Options tab. Under Layout, select 'Icon only'. Set Behaviour to 'Push', under State select 'Rollover'. Hit 'Choose icon'. In the 'navigation rollover images' folder, select rollover_image1.jpg. Hit Select and OK.

The top 10 Acrobat functions you need to know about...

01____**Edit PDFs**
There's little worse than exporting a PDF and noticing – even after all your checks! – a typo. Fortunately one essential tool in Acrobat 9 Pro is the ability to let you fix minor typographic errors. You can even edit and alter images in the PDF, and place images into it.

02____**Insert media into PDFs**
Insert a variety of multimedia into a PDF via Acrobat Pro Extended. Media can include Flash, QuickTime, MP3, MPEG and Windows Media files. Any computer that has Adobe Reader will be able to play these files.

03____**Paste into PDFs**
Paste anything from the computer's clipboard or InDesign into a new PDF document. Formatting and font choices will be preserved, so it fully retains the look of your original document.

04____**Create interactive PDFs of your website**
Why send a screenshot of your website for comments when you can convert it to a fully interactive PDF of the website? Animations,

graphics and links can all be seen and interacted with. Best of all, the Acrobat commenting tools can be used to review and mark up the site with comments and feedback.

05____**Work with Flash video within PDFs**
Drag and drop any video onto the Acrobat Pro Extended icon on your desktop, and Acrobat will open with the Insert dialog box. Acrobat will convert the video into the Flash video format for display within the PDF. You can then pause and add time-coded comments directly onto the PDF before you save the file and distribute it.

06____**Check file conformance to standards**
Clicking the PDF Info icon displays the Standards panel. If your client uses one of the default PDF/X presets, then you can easily check the files conformance to standards by using this tool.

07____**Send PDFs for review**
The 'Send by email for review' wizard enables you to send your PDF for email review by selecting email

addresses, previewing the invitation to review. Select the wizard by selecting Comments> Attach for Email review.

08____**Insert interactive buttons**
Liven up your presentations with interactive buttons. These can be made from JPEGs, GIFs and many other image formats. Be sure to remember that when using one of these formats the entire page is used, so crop the image or page to size first.

09____**Optimise your file size**
Under the Document menu you have the option to Reduce File Size. Here you can set Acrobat Version Compatibility. Optimising your file for later versions of Acrobat will enable a greater reduction in the file size.

10____**Enable mark-up tools**
You can now enable commenting and drawing mark-up tools for those viewing your PDFs in Acrobat Reader. Under the Advanced menu, select 'Enable Usage Rights in Adobe Reader'.

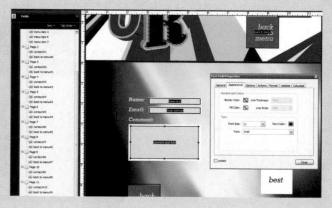

08____In Button Properties dialog, select 'Actions'. Choose Select Trigger: 'Mouse Down', then Select Action: 'Go to a page view'. Hit Add and select Page 1. In the 'Create Go to View' dialog, choose 'Set link'. Close Button Properties. Hook up remaining menu items to show their rollover images, and move to their pages.

09____Move to Page 13. Add an email form by selecting Forms>Add or Edit Fields. When asked 'Do you want Acrobat to detect the form fields for you?', select 'No' to enter Form Editing mode. From the 'Add New Field' drop-down, add a text field next to Name, Email and Comment by clicking next to each. Name accordingly.

10____Select each text field and double-click it to edit its properties. Under the Appearance tab, select a black border colour and a solid white fill colour. You can also set a font size here. We have used Arial at size 11.

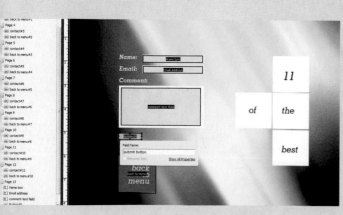

11____Remain in Forms Editing mode to add a Submit button to your form. From the 'Add a New Field' drop-down menu, select Button. Position the outlined button and click where you want it to be placed. Give it the field name 'Submit button'.

12____Double-click the grey button placeholder. In Button Properties, under Appearance change 'Fill color' to 'No color'. Under the Options tab Layout section select 'Icon only', set Behaviour set to 'Push', under State select 'Up', and then hit Choose Icon. Browse to submit_up.jpg then hit OK on the Select Icon box. Now highlight the Rollover state and hit Choose Icon. Select submit_over.jpg. Hit OK.

13____Select the Actions tab. For the Select Trigger option, select 'Mouse Down', and for Select Action choose 'Submit a form'. Hit the Add button. The Submit Form Selections box appears. Under 'Enter a URL for this link', enter mailto:[insert your email address here]. Click OK. Select the Close Form Editing button. Select File>Save to save the PDF for testing and distribution.

Pre-press agility with InDesign and Acrobat

Pre-press knowledge, the right tools and good communication will speed up the job and save you money. Here's how Acrobat can help

Preparing documents for the printing press used to be the domain of specialists in repro houses. That's not so often the case these days, as creatives have to play a part if they want the job to make it to the press smoothly and without incurring extra costs.

The first rule of press success is to communicate with your printer. You need to ensure that the files you will be sending aren't going to cause any unexpected hiccups on the way to the presses, as it's you that will be footing the bill for the printer's repro team to fix it. Get advice beforehand, and ensure you're clued up on the relevant technical information in advance.

InDesign CS4's Live Preflight feature does a pretty good job of keeping an eye on your documents as you work, but it can only be as reliable as the profile that it uses as a guide. Invest some time in getting to know this feature and defining profiles for all of your various output intents. You might even be lucky enough to have a printer who can supply you with a profile that you can simply import. If not, however, a small amount of co-operation will be in your common interest, as Nigel Cames of Evolve Print Management confirms.

"The reality today for designers and artworkers is that there's more to the job than just making it look great," says Cames. "They have to invest the time in making the job press-ready. They have great tools for the

job and should really get the most they can from them."

If you own Acrobat Professional (if you've bought Adobe's Creative Suite, it's in there), you've got an even more sophisticated toolset at your disposal. Some of these tools have functions that are beginning to rival even the dedicated applications used by repro specialists. Acrobat 9 Pro has an awesome print-production toolset that puts industrial-strength power in your hands. As Acrobat guru Jon Bessant says, you don't really need much else.

"People are often unaware that Acrobat provides them with almost everything they need to check, fix and deliver a solid, print-ready job," says Bessant. "It's a terrible shame that these killer features go undiscovered and designers remain largely in the dark about using them. There are resources and courses out there that can open up this whole area for those tasked with preparing artwork for print, and this can save you serious time and money." →

InDesign CS4, Acrobat 9 Pro

Make Acrobat your pre-press wizard

Tony Harmer puts an end to pre-press woes…

Tony Harmer
___ An Adobe-certified instructor holding over 40 certifications, and chapter leader for the London and Cardiff InDesign User Groups, Tony Harmer's 4T podcast is available on iTunes and at his site, www.tonyharmer.co.uk

Time needed
1 hour

Skills
___ Converting colours
___ Using the Ink Manager
___ Using Acrobat's Preflight
___ Embedding an Audit Trail

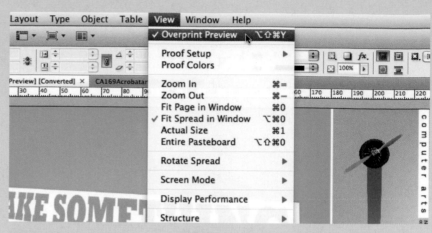

02_____Use Overprint Preview (Ctrl/Cmd+Alt/Opt+Shift+Y) to ensure that everything is as you would expect. This is especially important if you are using spot colours and/or any transparency in your artwork.

03_____Review your artwork using the Flattener Preview, especially in areas where text and graphics overlap. This is critical when transparency is involved, as you might find you need to move your text up onto its own layer.

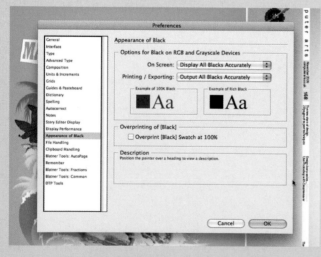

01_____Change your preferences in InDesign so that you can see any rich blacks that are present in your artwork. You'll find it listed under the 'Appearance of Black' category.

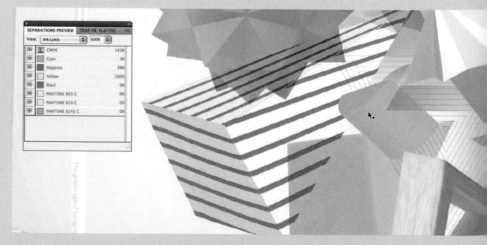

04_____Using information from your print provider or the process specifications, check the ink limits using the Ink Limits option from the drop-down in the Separations Preview. If you're printing web/gravure, you'll need to set this between 280% and 320%, for example.

Acrobat integration

Acrobat might be the final checking hub for all your PDFs destined for print, but the process can start as soon you begin work on your document. Your Creative Suite colour settings can be synchronised between Acrobat, InDesign, Photoshop and Illustrator to ensure that your workflow is perfectly colour-managed from the start. Remember that you need to use all the tools at your disposal to ensure that you're supplying your printer with the best possible PDF file. If you're making changes to your source file, it is often safer to re-export the changed pages and then send those to your printer. If you rely on the printer to make the changes, it'll still be you that gets it in the neck if there's an error.

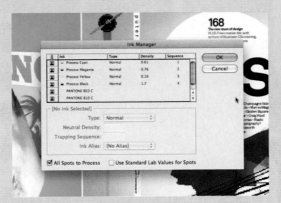

05_____ If you have spot colours in your artwork but intend to print the job as four-colour, use the Ink Manager (found in the Swatches panel menu) to convert them. You can also change the trapping order of your inks in this dialog, but only do so under advice.

06_____ The new Object Inspector in the Output Preview panel enables you to click and view detailed information about objects used in your artwork, such as resolution, colour, transparency and more. The panel also enables you to view separations and set warning colours for overprinting and rich black.

Top five
Acrobat preferences

01 Overprint Preview
Acrobat's Overprint Preview is by default set for PDF/X files, but can be changed to 'always'.

02 Show Art, Trim & Bleed Boxes
This shows the trim of your artwork (green box) and the bleed (blue box). It's invaluable!

03 Enhance Thin Lines
Strangely, turning this off will normalise fat L and I characters typically seen from outlined text.

04 Smooth Line Art
Turn this one off if you see inexplicable thin lines around flattened objects and shadows.

05 Enable Text Word-wrapping
This little-known touch-up feature can be turned on or off as required to enable better editing of text paragraphs.

07_____ The Convert Colours dialog box does exactly what the name suggests and boasts some great features. You can match various criteria and choose different conversion attributes. Conversion goodies available include preserving black and promoting grey to CMYK black on individual pages or the whole document.

08_____ The Ink Manager enables the mapping of a spot colour to a different spot or process colour, achieved by creating an ink alias. This is really useful if you have more than one copy of a spot (perhaps introduced by placed files) or if the file contains too many spots.

10_____ If you've run a final preflight inspection in Acrobat, you could embed an Audit Trail. This works like a wrapper for the document, complete with a signature from Acrobat, and contains metadata that shows that when the file left you it conformed to a standard.

09_____ Use Acrobat's Preflight to detect any potential problems. InDesign is good but Acrobat is much better. You can also use Snap View to view problem objects – just select 'Show in Snap' from the bottom of the Preflight window.

1&1 Web Hosting
SUCCESS
1&1 Premium Features Drive Traffic

"Our website is the first point of contact we have with many of our customers and it's an essential part of our business. 1&1 hosting packages offer great value for money and are extremely flexible. Creating our website was an easy process, with the 1&1 hosting package you have the freedom to make your website into what you want it to be and create a professional image."

Ian Parley, www.taste-buds.co.uk

Go to www.1and1.co.uk for many other fantastic offers.

MEMBER OF
united internet

Call **0871 641 21 21**   Calls cost 6p per minute from a BT landline, calls from other operators and mobiles may be higher.

PetPunk
—Founded by illustrator Gediminas Šiaulys (far left) and animator Andrius Kirvela back in 2005, Lithuanian design studio PetPunk has been at the forefront of the country's post-communist cultural renaissance.

A fusion of western and eastern design and social trends, PetPunk's work includes posters, books and short films, and has achieved acclaim across the globe. The studio won the 2009 ADC Young Guns competition. www.petpunk.com

PetPunk

The Lithuanian capital is in the middle of a cultural resurgence. **Charlotte West** talks to Vilnius-based illustration and motion graphics studio PetPunk about bringing its Soviet past together with its European future

In Europe and the United States, Crayola crayons are a staple in kids' creative lives; Burnt Sienna brushes shoulders with Brick Red, while Teal Blue and Mulberry retire to make room for Wild Blue Yonder and Mango Tango. But what if your childhood palette was limited to black, brown, blue, green, yellow and something that resembles red? How would this shape your visual world view?

For Lithuanian animation studio PetPunk, made up of illustrator Gediminas Šiaulys and animator Andrius Kirvela, the result has been a strange marriage of eastern European sensibilities and folk art with modern, almost post-punk visuals. PetPunk's unique angle hasn't gone unnoticed either – in October 2009 the studio picked up the 2009 Art Directors Club Young Guns Award, which recognises the body of work of designers under 30.

Bloc colours

As 20-somethings, the pair straddle two vastly different realms of experience. They grew up under Communism, but were teenagers when Lithuania gained independence from the Soviet Union in 1992. "We had a dual experience of cultures," says Šiaulys. "A lot of our work is an investigation into our childhood, a childhood where there wasn't any advertising. This visual clash of two worlds – Socialism vs Capitalism – is reflected in our aesthetic approach. We mix totally different visual styles and techniques."

Take, for instance, their recent project 'Carousel' – a limited-edition giclée print on canvas – and the intro for an independent film they're working on ("about warm love in cold winter's day," according to Šiaulys). The piece is a 3D rendering that interprets the opening

credits of a famous Soviet children's television show the pair watched as kids. It was created using an effect that mimics brush strokes and is caused by insufficient computing data. PetPunk has, in essence, turned an error into a work of art, which they say celebrates "computer art at its full, natural, digital beauty".

Šiaulys and Kirvela met while working on a commercial project at a web design agency. After working on several projects with other young Lithuanian artists, they discovered that their diverse skillsets meshed well and decided to start their own studio. But while the duo employs thoroughly modern techniques, they don't forget where they came from. Kirvela describes the five decades of Socialism following World War II as years of terror, censorship, propaganda, Russification and a permanent shortage of goods. "This created poor conditions to develop people's consciousness and creativity. Any departure from the norm was strictly kept down by governmental structures. The situation for design was also difficult. There was no free market, no competition and almost no advertising. This was our childhood," he says.

For graphic designers, Kirvela explains, there was only one outlet for artistic self-expression – posters. "Since designers were separated from the world's modern tendencies, their inspiration came from ethno-art or the work of pre-war artists, as well as from other socialist countries like Poland and Czechoslovakia."

After independence in 1992, Lithuania experienced an influx of culture and goods from the west, which threatened to eclipse its national identity. "Capitalism stood up with all its weight, but society wasn't ready. The culture →

01

02

01 PetPunk gave a nod to the Surrealist movement in its art direction and design for Lithuanian band **Biplan**'s *Nuodai* album artwork

02 The austere opening credits to a Soviet-era children's show was the inspiration for this limited-edition giclée print, entitled **'Carousel'**

03 **'Apocalypse'**, one of a series of illustrations produced for the Effigy clothing ad campaign that was art directed and designed by PetPunk

03

We don't have an established aesthetic… in our world there is no 'right' way. That gives us a lot of freedom

Andrius Kirvela

04 A still from *Let There Be Night*, the short that scooped a slew of awards, including Gold in the Lithuanian Ad Awards Adrenalinas 2008

05 PetPunk is dipping its toes into the world of illustrated products, one of the first being the **'Tie' pair of pillowcases**, available to buy through the PetPunk website

06 'Balandis' was PetPunk's illustrated contribution to the Shift 2008 Calendar

04

05

06

07

Studio profile
PetPunk

07 Stills from **The Magnificent Town of Vilnius**, the PetPunk short commissioned to celebrate Vilnius's status as European Capital of Culture 2009

08 Animated piece **Legends of Exos** was produced for the PSST!3 collaboration. Šiaulys oversaw the character designs, while Kirvela worked on the general design and animation

09 PetPunk expertly walks the line between **intricate illustrative elements** and **pared-down cool**. Everyday products such as brown paper bags make the perfect canvas for its works

A day in the life of Gediminas Šiaulys PetPunk art director and co-founder

8am My little daughter Ursula wakes me up shouting "Kakooo! Kakoooo!" That means she wants to poo.

9am Prepare breakfast and watch *Pocoyo* while mommy is still sleeping.

10am Sit in studio. Check out Hi-Fructose, Juxtapoz, FFFFOUND! and spend a little bit of time on Facebook (just a little, I promise!).

11am Play Sigur Rós. Answer emails, interviews and try to concentrate on what I have to do today. Got invitation to give a lecture at SRF conference in Bergen. Google Bergen. Thinking of going there, and taking my wife and daughter.

11:30am Short chat with our beloved reps Hornet Inc on upcoming things. Planning the trip to ADC Young Guns Awards in New York with Andrius.

1pm Deliver our 'Carousel' canvas to a gallery. Then lunch with my lovely wife Elena.

2:30pm Go to Lithuanian Ethnographic museum to get material and inspiration from handicraft masks to build masks for PetPunk. Saw some interesting sculptures. Should I go with wood or bronze?

4pm Drawing art boards for our upcoming short film *Little Angels*. Working on the winter mood for 'Soviet childhood'. Drawing concrete blocks, frozen playground, snow and snowflakes. Still a lot of compositioning work to be done.

7pm Go home. Go crazy with daughter: build towers, hide and seek, sing songs, dance, scream, jump, swing, destroy books, crash plates and so on.

9pm Finally Ursula's batteries are off. I should draw a moustache under her nose while she sleeps. A surprise for the morning!

9.30pm Check out some books. Draw illustrations for the *The Magnificent Town of Vilnius* book in my sketchpad.

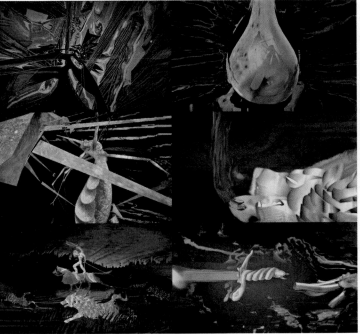

08

09

→ Cultural divides

Like Lithuanian society at large, the PetPunk team have had to reconcile their Soviet past with ambitions for the future, exploring their home country's national identity in the process. For example, in *The Magnificent City of Vilnius*, a video animation for the European Capital of Culture 2009 campaign, PetPunk explores the history, multiculturalism and creativity of the Lithuanian capital. Inspired both by Lithuanian mythology and viral pet videos on YouTube, the animation presents a dreamy, almost childlike universe populated by animal-headed denizens. Like many of PetPunk's projects, the final product is charming, if a bit rough around the edges.

But that's the way it's supposed to be. Kirvela and Šiaulys revel in the gory details of their work, taking their time to enjoy the creative process. They are also more than willing to share the messier side of the production process with the world, such as uploading to Flickr the amusing behind-the-scenes takes of the parade of pets that came through the studio during the filming of *The Magnificent City of Vilnius*.

Describing their work as "hybrid and chaotic" and "a bit distracting," Kirvela says experimentation and improvisation are hallmarks of the PetPunk design process: "We don't have an established aesthetic. We find the errors in our creative process. Something goes wrong, and the result is really interesting. We actually use that as our technique. It might be unprofessional, but in our world there is no 'right' way to do it. That gives us a lot of freedom."

Kirvela says that in *The Magnificent City of Vilnius* animation he used an effect designed for an entirely different purpose to "grow" the buildings and trees. Some of the scenes were also created by mixing 3D objects with the 2D drawings – an idea that only came about during the animation process. PetPunk takes a similar mash-up approach to computer graphics, as Šiaulys points out: "[They] often tend to be stylised and perfect. We prefer warmer and imperfect."

Another example of what Kirvela describes as "unintended effects" is a recent clip PetPunk has made for *PSST! 3*, a collaborative short film project done by international teams made up of designers, directors and animators. He says he used a "video compression error effect to achieve painterly surfaces while still keeping it purely digital, without trying to replicate or simulate real-world painting techniques."

While much of the visual material and animation coming out of digital studios today appears seamless, it is in the flaws that PetPunk finds its own sense of perfection. Kirvela says he takes inspiration from contemporary Japanese motion graphics works precisely because of their quirks. "To me, it looks like there are lots of artists who are not bound by execution standards and trying to do 'good-looking' stuff. They play hard, experiment, break and invent rules," he says. It sounds like he might just be describing PetPunk.

coming from the west was so rich, colourful and attractive that it drowned everything local. The adjective 'Lithuanian' became a synonym for poor quality or a lack of originality," Kirvela recalls.

In the last decade and a half, the country has morphed from a totalitarian political regime and centrally planned economy to democracy and a free market, complete with plenty of growing pains. The utter transformation – and concurrent identity crisis – of this tiny Baltic nation culminated with its entry to the European Union in 2004.

Unrecognisable
pixart.it
easy printing
48hours from now!
Instantaneous quotation and order at: www.pixart.it - *92% of the orders received in the morning

...since they print long runs with **pixart.it**

Open studios

Their output decorates our streets, covers our television screens and occupies our homes, but what inhabits the space behind the doors of the world's design studios? We explore the creative sanctuaries of some of today's most influential designers

▶ **Blue River, Newcastle, UK**
www.blueriver.co.uk
Blue River is in a historic hot spot. Originally a foundry, the Newcastle studio was the birthplace of some of the very first locomotive technology. "In fact," reveals creative director Anthony Cantwell, "George Stephenson's workshop – the birthplace of the Rocket – is just round the corner from us."

The space pictured is the studio's "supposed quiet area". This is where everyone gravitates when they need a little space to think. It's also one of office pooch Badger's favourite hangouts. He's always here, ready to act as a distraction, helping to de-stress everyone and get them focussed on the job in hand.

◀▼ **Love Creative, Manchester, UK**
www.lovecreative.com

At Manchester's Love Creative, the bosses sit behind an emergency access panel. "We can 'break the glass' should we need a shoulder to cry on or anything else," explains PR manager Lisa Hughes. The dart board, on the other hand, "is for good old fashioned fun and relaxation."

The plates on the wall are all chosen by Love people, so they represent everyone at the studio, old and new. "When someone leaves, the dates of their time at Love – and their plate – are left on the wall as a memory of them," says Hughes.

◀ **Homework, Copenhagen, Denmark**
www.homework.dk
"My work environment means a great deal to me,"
says Homework's Jack Dahl. "[I like] light, calmness
and clean desk space." This may sound strange
given what you see on the left, and Dahl
acknowledges this: "I know that the images tell
another story, but these days Homework is
moving. So, to be honest with you, there's is quite a
lot of portfolio references around, research, files
and folders."

While the move progresses, work
continues – on a Takashi Murakami monograph for
Galerie Emmanuel Perrotin and Carolina Herrera
perfume packaging, among other things. "We will
clean up on Friday," Dahl promises.

▼ **Sensomatic, Vienna, Austria**
www.sensomatic.com
The Sensomatic team works from a ground floor
studio in Vienna's second district. The space opens
onto a back yard containing a wild garden, which
Christine Zmoelnig and Florian Koch enjoy tending
when the mood takes them.

"We use our terrace in summer and
take work breaks mowing the lawn, watering plants
and removing leaves from our roof," says Koch.
Inside, the rear wall is used as a pin board for work
and inspiration. "We drew wires across it, which we
use like a clothesline," explains Koch. "We change
the display constantly."

▶ **Sawdust, London, UK**
www.madebysawdust.co.uk
"Our current building used to be an old dance school," says Sawdust's Rob Gonzalez. "It's very warehouse-like – big windows, open spaces, wooden floors."

Surrounded by the galleries and cafes of Hoxton, in a building shared with fashion, music and web companies, Sawdust enjoys the archetypal creative setting. On Gonzalez's desk is "an iMac, Wacom, telephone, keys, mandatory cup of tea, squared sketch pad, and our one window."

And, peeking out from just towards the left of Gonzalez's screen is Felix, the studio's cat, who is made of metal and has marbles for eyes.

◀ **Loft Digital, London, UK**
www.loftdigital.com
Loft is not a big agency. The team doesn't believe you need an army of talent at your back – "You just need smart people with plenty of get-up-and-go, and a fun environment," says designer Clare Sutcliffe. Director Nick Nettleton, project manager Woody Sabran and Sutcliffe work together from their Clerkenwell HQ, which is a huge, open-plan space shared with 10 other small companies all working in design and digital. Four more full-timers dial in from around the world.

The walls are covered in cards and posters collected over the years, mainly by Sutcliffe. There's everything from '20s Moroccan travel posters to eBoy work. "Somewhere in there," she adds, "are some linocuts of London landmarks by Paul Catherall, which I particularly like."

◀ **Fi, Stockholm, Sweden**
www.f-i.com
Fantasy Interactive has two offices: one in New York, the other in Stockholm. Every week in NYC, reveals interactive designer Johnny Michaelsen, "the entire team gathers around the large dining table for a sophisticated round of wine tasting and a great time-out."

Meanwhile, in a newly renovated attic space in the heart of Stockholm (pictured left), laidback meetings nestle down next to outbursts of creative effervescence boiling over from a games room, equipped with pool table, foosball and multiple gaming consoles.

▼ **magneticNorth, Manchester, UK**
www.mnatwork.com
The mN team has been at 101 Princess Street in Manchester for three years, in an office designed to showcase the mN ethos which is, says marketing director Kate Towey, "centred around play, engagement and curiosity."

Installing the Moooi Dear Ingo lamp in the reception area meant re-enforcing the ceiling so that those sitting in the lovely Eames DAR chair below could do so safely. It's a comfortable place to enjoy the studio's excellent library, the expansion of which can be followed at mnlibrary.tumblr.com.

▼ **Studio Parris Wakefield, Suffolk, UK**
www.parriswakefield.com
"We moved out of London to our 18th century barn in 2006," says creative director Howard Wakefield. "The vast openness of the surrounding commonland gave us room to breathe and an apparent blank canvas, free of connotations." This is a logic the studio endeavours to apply to its creative output.

      Contemporary furniture complements the craftsmanship of the original building – iMac, Moroso, Eames and Aeron sit perfectly with gnarled oak – and the modern remains true to its heritage. "This is another aspect of our work," adds Wakefield. "We feel honesty is paramount."

▲ **Intro, London, UK**
www.intro-uk.com
It has taken years to build Intro's collection of analogue and digital ephemera, design books and artworks to this precipitous state. "It's the accumulated detritus from various shoots we've done and bits of kit I've picked up along the way,"

says the studio's design director, Mat Cook.
Old drum machines, vision mixers, lots of analogue and rare equipment – the wall is ever evolving. "It's much pillaged. It's a working pile of crap," says Cook. But, he insists, it isn't pure decoration: "There's definitely something in there. It's a living mass."

▼ Kemistry, London, UK
www.kemistry.co.uk

When Kemistry moved to Shoreditch in 2002, studio founders Ricky Churchill and Graham McCallum had a moment of inspiration or, admits McCallum, "pub madness, depending on how you look at it." They decided that since their new premises were in one of the most up-and-coming creative areas of London, it would be a good idea to turn the ground floor into a gallery, as shown below.

"We wanted the exhibitions to concentrate on design rather than fine art," says McCallum, "and to feature the work of people who inspire us and will hopefully inspire others." Below, James Joyce is seen hanging his show.

▶ No Pattern, Illinois, USA
www.nopattern.com

"I love surrounding myself with things that inspire me, without overdoing it," says designer and illustrator Chuck Anderson. Work by Dave Kinsey, KAWS, Deanne Cheuk and Mike Perry sits alongside drum kits and a selection of comfortable, classic seating: "Herman Miller Aeron and plywood chairs – a must have," says Anderson.

Anderson's 30-inch Apple display gives him the visual real estate to do whatever he wants creatively, and his drums "are great for getting out energy built up by frustrating clients." The black and white table is a collaboration between Anderson and Lars Amhoff of Kinkyform.com.

▼ Form, London, UK
www.form.uk.com

Form's Paul West supplied us with a key to what he calls his "organised mess". We only have space for the bottom row, so you'll have to try to identify the rest yourself...

Pictured left to right: postcard of Joseph Crawhall's 'The White Drake'; snowboarding photos; various keyrings; James Jarvis *Zombie* figures; Berlin's Trabant cars; Pete Fowler *Monsterism* figures; 'Design Wank' UniForm promotional beer mats; Philip's Planisphere; Font frames; 'Leave It All Behind' Ruby Foo self promotion screen-print on wood base.

◀Segura Inc, Chicago, USA
www.segura-inc.com
Carlos Segura's building in Chicago's
Bucktown district is "pretty unique". A
former bank, it has feeling of solidity that is
hard to miss. And, deep within this
imposing setting, Segura has himself quite
a spot.

"I spend my days in my very
large office," he says contentedly – an
office so large, in fact, that throughout the
years there have been no less than five
motorcycles in situ, plus a full drum kit
(pictured) and a variety of other
distractions. "It is my personal retreat,"
adds Segura. "I am completely alone all
day; just the way I like it."

▶ :phunk studio, Singapore
www.phunkstudio.com

"A glimpse of the private space where pugilistic heroes come together to exchange their martial arts moves" – this is :phunk studio, says Alvin Tan.

:phunk studio might be Singapore's creative powerhouse but, says Tan, "we would like to think of this space as a sanctum that is at times framed by a form of chaos; the formative time when you are working out what is the next thing to do and how to do it – a work in progress under control."

▼ DED Associates, Sheffield, UK
www.dedass.com

The DED Associates team seems to enjoy the process as much as the outcome. "Never knowing what it will be from one day to the next is the best way to describe our space," says creative director Nik Daughtry. "From artist studio to design studio and back again; these are the two sides of our shiny existence."

The space does not define the people, rather it is defined by what DED Associates does within it, and when. "The space itself sometimes feels like home and sometimes feels like hell," Daughtry adds, "but it's ours and we create here."

Can't get enough of behind-the-scenes studio insights? Every issue we continue to tour a spectacular design studio in our Studio of the Month feature, which you will find in the Output section.

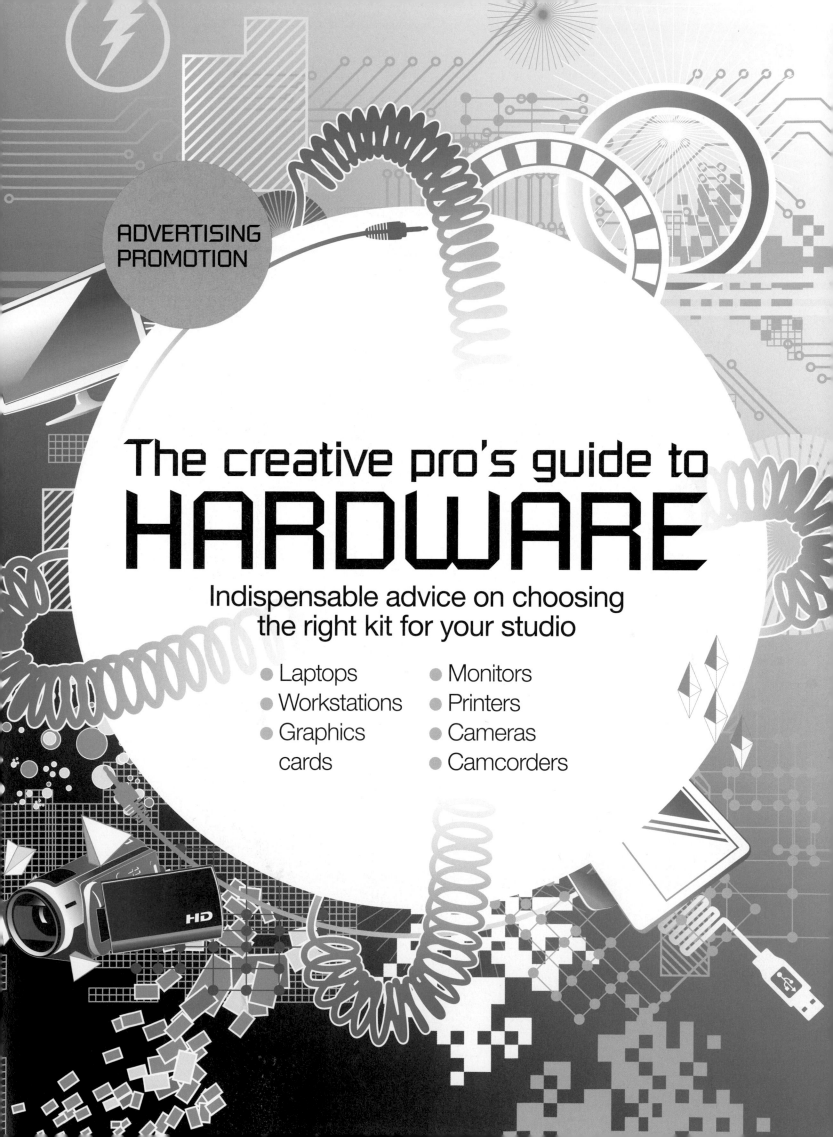

The creative pro's guide to HARDWARE

Indispensable advice on choosing the right kit for your studio

- Laptops
- Workstations
- Graphics cards
- Monitors
- Printers
- Cameras
- Camcorders

dabs⊙com

500GB Samsung
Portable Hard Drive

With Terminator Salvation pre-loaded

With an elegant, high gloss front cover combined with luxurious leather like reverse side, Samsung's S series complements your style. A sophisticated pattern on the cover is the essence of the sleek and modern design. The compact S2 Portable - which fits in a pocket - is an ideal storage solution for those who want to carry massive amounts of digital content whilst on the run.

TERMINATOR SALVATION

500GB PORTABLE HARDDRIVE

SAMSUNG

500GB PORTABLE HARDDRIVE 12

Only

£69

2.5" FORM FACTOR

HIGH SPEED USB 2.0

FULL LENGTH MOVIE PRE-LOADED READY TO WATCH!

COLUMBIA PICTURES • THE HALCYON COMPANY • SONY PICTURES

Buy it now at www.dabs.com/3dworld

 20,000 Computing & electronics products online

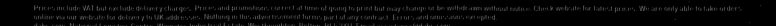

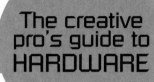

The creative
pro's guide to
HARDWARE

Contents

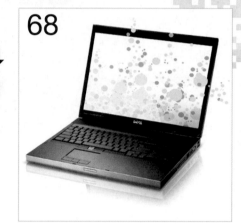

68

64 **Ideal set-ups**
Creative toolkit essentials, whatever your
digital design specialism

68 **Laptops**
Strike a balance between power and
portability for your perfect laptop

71 **Workstations**
Why you can't beat a desktop for high
performance and bespoke specs

74 **Graphics cards**
Power up pro-style for everything from 3D
rendering to video editing

76 **The DX11 revolution**
AMD outlines what DX11 means
to the 3D creative industry

78 **Monitors**
The dramatic differences between
mid-market and high-end explained

79 **Digital SLRs**
Capture images like a pro with our guide to
the most suitable DSLR for you

81 **Printers**
Whether it produces proofs, paperwork or
posters, a quality printer is a studio must

82 **Camcorders**
Reduce post-production efforts with a HD
camera that delivers high-quality footage

71

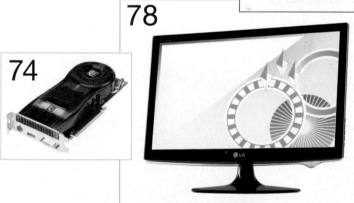

78

74

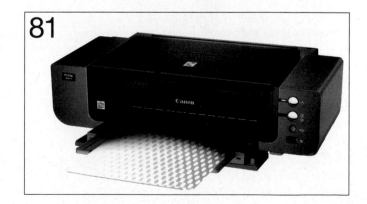

81

Choose the right set-up

Helping you pick the right kit for your creative needs

Selecting the right hardware set-up for your needs is critical in the field of digital art and design. The likes of Photoshop, Painter and 3D creation applications such as Cinema 4D and 3ds Max are powerful programs, and require a suitably powerful hardware set-up.

For mobile needs, a high-spec laptop is key. Screen size, CPU power and RAM capacity are all factors that determine how creative applications perform. And while a portable may be fine for Photoshop and digital painting applications, it won't offer the productive clout of a bespoke desktop.

For desktop-bound workstations, power is key, and for video editors and 3D artists the biggest, most powerful rig you can afford is generally recommended. High-end set-ups can reach into the thousands of pounds, but can handle large renders and video edits with ease. Smaller, less powerful machines are fine for RAM-intensive applications like Photoshop, however, so determining your individual needs and buying a machine to suit is by far the best course of action.

How you view your work in progress is just as important as the kit you create it on. Sitting in front of a 19-inch monitor simply won't cut it in creative work, and investing in the biggest monitor you can afford is not only better on your eyes but will actively make you more productive. What's more, if you're a video editor or 3D artist with high-end needs, a widescreen display is a must. If you work in a colour critical print environment, a professionally calibrated monitor will help to prevent any printing errors.

With your core set-up established, a range of peripherals will help to speed up the creative process. Whether you're printing roughs, samples or collectable artworks, a solid studio printer is a must. Outsourcing is fine for professional longer runs, but for real creative control an A3 workhorse printer with multiple inks and media options should be included in any set-up.

A graphics tablet is especially pertinent to digital painters and designers. The likes of Wacom and Genius offer a range fit for any budget, with high-end A3 models costing anything up to £1000 while smaller consumer options such as Wacom's Bamboo series are available for far less. If you're a digital painter or designer, a tablet can, after a bit of getting used to, truly speed up your workflow and revolutionise the way you create your work.

Many digital designers rely on capturing their own reference imagery and assets with a digital camera. There are hundreds of options available, from pocket-slim point-and-shoots to professional digital SLRs totalling thousands of pounds. Sites like www.photoradar.com can help you in selecting a model suited to your own creative needs.

Similarly, video editors will need hardware to capture their footage on. Whether they're working with a compact camcorder or professional HD cameras with a professional price tag, something that shoots to hard disk and can be easily transferred to your studio set-up is key.

With all of this taken into account, you can achieve the perfect creative hardware set-up. Look at your needs and, armed with our buying advice, streamline your creative processes. ■

The ideal set-up...

For digital painters and illustrators

Digital painters and illustrators rely on RAM-intensive applications such as Adobe's Photoshop and Illustrator, and Corel's Painter, and so a well-equipped laptop or workstation is a must for a fast creation process.

A large monitor will really benefit digital artists, especially when paired with a graphics tablet. This forms a killer combination, enabling you to sketch naturally and see your work vividly and accurately.

What you need:	Optional Extras:
Laptop with 2GB of RAM	Graphics tablet
Widescreen monitor	A3+ printer
Digital camera/SLR	

For web and print designers

Like illustrators and digital painters, web and print designers depend on RAM-heavy applications like Photoshop and Illustrator. Pair this with the CPU demands of Flash and any coding created in Dreamweaver, and a fast workstation is the way to go. Similarly, a widescreen monitor is a must for web and print designers, with the print workers and retouchers in particular benefitting from colour-accurate models.

What you need:	Optional Extras:
Workstation with	Graphics tablet
8GB RAM	A3+ printer
High-end graphics card	Digital camera/SLR
Widescreen monitor	

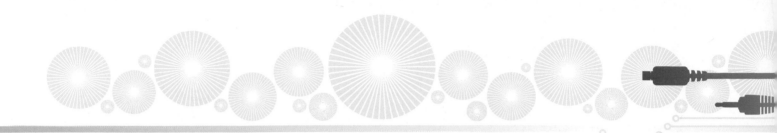

The ideal set-up... [cont'd]

For 3D artists

3D artists and designers have some of the most demanding hardware requirements of all the creative industries. A workstation for tasks such as animation, rendering and digital sculpting needs a lot of RAM and a quick processor, preferably capable of multi-threading across multiple cores. A widescreen monitor is a must here, too, particularly for grading or detailed colouring work. Finally, a graphics tablet can speed your workflow considerably, so experiment with one in your preferred applications to see if it can save you time, effort and, ultimately, money.

What you need:	**Optional Extras:**
Workstation with	Graphics tablet
8GB RAM	A3+ printer
Widescreen monitor	Digital camera/SLR

For video and motion graphics editors

Video editing applications like Premiere, After Effects and Final Cut Studio are resource heavy, so a powerful workstation set-up is a must. Similarly, a widescreen monitor or dual monitor set-up is recommended. Products such as Nvidia's Quadro range have extended GPU features for faster video processing, while the device you choose to capture your footage on is key, so opt for the best your budget will stretch to.

What you need:	**Optional Extras:**
Workstation with	Graphics tablet
8GB RAM	A3+ printer
High-end graphics card	Digital camera/SLR
Widescreen monitor	
HD camcorder	

Windows®. Life without Walls™. Dell recommends Windows 7.

DELL PRECISION M6500

WORK AT THE SPEED OF THOUGHT

The new Dell Precision™ M6500 mobile workstations are the preferred choice for professionals who need workstation performance on-the-go. Optimized and certified for Industry leading software applications; and configurable with NVIDIA® Quadro® FX graphics solutions, the Dell Precision M6500 delivers outstanding application performance, lightning fast rendering and excellent value.

CLICK OR CALL

Visit: www.dell.co.uk/precision or

☎ 0844 444 3252

www.nvidia.co.uk/quadro

Choose the right...

Laptop

Choosing the right mobile workstation for you is all about balancing power and portability

A high-spec, powerful laptop is essential for any creative professional. Whether you're a web designer, digital painter, 3D artist, graphic designer or all four, a powerful mobile workstation is an incredibly important addition to your arsenal. Due to the power of modern laptops, in some circumstances it may even be that you can ditch the desktop machine completely, leaving a monitor, external keyboard and mouse/tablet on your desk when you need a bit more desktop real estate.

Choosing the right laptop for your needs is easy. As with desktop machines, it begins with the choice between Mac and PC. Then you need to work out what size screen you want, which is usually a decision between a more portable 15-inch machine or a 17-inch powerhouse. Similarly, check out the maximum resolution; for serious creative work, 1440x900 pixels is sufficient, anything bigger being a matter of personal preference. And has it got a brighter, greener LED display?

The machine's graphics card is also vitally important – anything with less than 256MB of video RAM should be avoided. Always maxing out the RAM of your machine is vital to performance gains, with 8GB becoming increasingly common practice. In terms of hard drives – especially if you're going to be doing video and 3D work – the bigger, and faster, the better (a 500GB, 7200rpm drive would be fine for most work). You could also consider a solid state drive if it's available as a build-to-order option, although prices are high and

capacities relatively low. One of the more simple decisions is the processor – most modern laptops have a dual-core set-up, with newer machines (like the Dell M6500 opposite) featuring quad-core processors.

Battery life should also be looked at very carefully, along with whether or not it is user-replaceable. Finally, make sure it has all the ports you need – is your old FireWire 400 drive or camcorder going to hook up, for instance? Or will it drive your huge monitor? If you're a video pro, has it got the audio connectivity you need?

Whatever your needs as a creative pro, the ultimate decision lies in balancing the power and portability of the laptop you need with the budget you have. ■

In focus
Dell M6500

The new mobile workhouse from Dell delivers an incredible amount of power to the creative professional

Simply put, the Dell Precision M6500 is one of the most powerful portable machines you can currently get your hands on – and a raft of customisation options makes it highly versatile for the creative professional wanting the best performance possible from a laptop. All things considered though, this is a desktop replacement.

Weighing 3.86kg, this is not a machine you'll want to be taking everywhere with you. But then again, it is still a portable computer, albeit a large and extremely powerful one, and can therefore be moved from studio to studio if needs be.

With the top-spec M6500 (it comes in a number of configurations) featuring a quad-core CPU, the ability to house 16GB RAM, up to 1.5TB of storage, an Nvidia Quadro FX 3800M graphics card with 1GB of dedicated memory and a 17-inch LED display, there's no doubting that this is a true creative workhorse.

Taking centre stage is a lightning Intel Core i7-920XM quad-core 2.0GHz processor, which is upgradable to the Extreme edition. This, coupled with 4GB RAM as standard, makes rendering times for both video and 3D

projects – along with Photoshop and other multi-threaded app operations – extremely speedy. Of course, maxing it out to 16GB is going to improve things further. The ability to have up to three storage devices (two HDDs and an SSD mini-card) configured in RAID makes it even more versatile for video pros wanting a portable editing suite. You can even add a multi-touch trackpad with jog shuttle.

Of course, the display on a mobile workstation is vitally important, and the M6500 doesn't disappoint, with a 17-inch, super-bright LED display configurable as an edge-to-edge screen with up to 1920x1200 for working with HD content. The Nvidia Quadro graphics card is pretty special, too – workstation-class and capable of the most demanding 3D work. Although it's not a hugely portable machine, the M6500 is well-built and extremely powerful.

Whilst we'd mainly recommend the Dell M6500 to video editors, motionographers and 3D artists, digital painters and image editing pros will also find it hugely beneficial to their productivity.
www.dell.co.uk

The Dell M6500 at a glance

PRICE: From £1652
CPU: Up to Intel Core i7-920XM quad-core Extreme processors
RAM: Up to 16GB 1333MHz DDR3
DISPLAY: 17-inch LED
RES: Up to 1920x1200
HDD: Support for one, two or three storage devices with optional RAID0, RAID1 or RAID5 configurations
GRAPHICS: Up to Nvidia Quadro FX 3800M Graphics with 1GB dedicated memory
WEIGHT: 3.86kg
DIMENSIONS: 393mm (w) x 280.5mm (d) x 34.5mm (h)

INFINITE Possibilities...

Workstation Specialists

+44 (0) 800 180 4801
sales@wksmail.com

www.workstationspecialists.com

As a leading UK manufacturer of 3D graphics workstations and rendering systems, we have a special understanding of the 3D industry and are able to offer a bespoke portfolio of products individually tuned and optimised for YOUR creative projects and workflow.

Maximizing performance, power efficiency and optimizing total cost of ownership.

Choose the right...

Workstation

For unrivalled performance, customisation and future upgrade ease, you can't beat a desktop for creative work

For digital designers, illustrators and artists, the core specifications to look for in a new desktop workstation are needs-dependent. The likes of Photoshop, Flash and Painter rely on fast-firing RAM for working with large documents and powerful tools – so a well specified desktop should carry at least 8GB of on-board RAM.

Couple this with a multi-core processor set-up, and even the most layer-heavy PSD will open with ease. Multi-core processors enable highly threaded applications to run more processes in parallel, and for 3D artists multi-core processing also aids in rendering times. Intel's i7 line is a quad-core chipset with processor speeds of between 1.6GHz and 3.47GHz, while AMD's latest 'Istanbul' chipsets are six-core processors.

When it comes to output, a top-flight graphics card is required, especially if you're working in 3D or with video. Nvidia's latest Quadro FX range was developed with Adobe CS4 in mind, and will aid 3D artists working on large renders too. With high specs for video and high frame rate support, gaming cards such as ATI's Radeon 4000 series cards are also great for creative work.

A super fast RAID array is preferable for hefty creative work, while form factor is a personal choice. With Macs now able to boot into Windows as well as OS X, PC-only software (such as 3ds Max) doesn't limit you to a PC. But, Mac Pros are comparably expensive to the likes of Dell, HP and other mainstream manufacturers. The other option is to go to a specialist, such as Workstation Specialists, to get a high-end machine perfectly optimised for your workflow. ∎

Three of the best... workstations
The desktop machines at the heart of your workflow

What: Dell T1500, £645.08 (incl. VAT)
Why: Intel Core i7 2.93GHz quad-core processor, 8GB RAM (up to 16GB supported), Nvidia Quadro FX580 graphics card, 2x250GB SATA HD in RAID 0
Where: www.dell.co.uk

What: Mac Pro, £1,899 (incl. VAT)
Why: Intel Xeon 2.66GHz quad-core, 3GB RAM (up to 16GB supported), 640GB hard drive, Nvidia GeForce GT 120 with 512MB
Where: www.apple.com/uk/macpro

What: Workstation Specialists WSX114, £3049.12 (incl. VAT)
Why: Workstation Enhanced Intel Core i7 64-bit quad-core processor, 12GB RAM (up to 24GB supported), Ultra High Performance 120GB hard disk drive (SATA2 - SSD), Nvidia Quadro FX3800 1.0GB
Where: www.workstationspecialists.com

IMAGINE. CREATE. SHARE.

HP SkyRoom

Buy any HP Z400, Z600 or Z800 Workstation/ TFT bundles and save £150 on RRP price, plus you can claim a free SkyRoom Accessory Kit worth £92!*

HP Z-Series Workstations now come pre-installed with HP SkyRoom video-conferencing software. With HP SkyRoom you can interact freely with up to three colleagues across the globe simultaneously. You can also share live audio, video, applications and streaming media - such as 3D engineering models or feature film dailies - through your PC.

HP Z400 Workstation + HP LP2275w 22" Widescreen LCD Monitor

- Intel® Xeon® Processor W3520
- Genuine Windows® 7 Professional
- 4GB memory
- 500GB hard drive
- DVD±RW
- HP SkyRoom software.

RRP Price £1499.99 Inc VAT

Promo Bundle Price £1349.99 Inc VAT

Saving £150!

Order: AL165111

PLUS CLAIM A FREE
SkyRoom Accessory Kit*
- Logitech® Quickcam® Pro
- 9000 USB Camera Audio
- Headset with boom and microphone

VISIT: misco.co.uk/go/hpworkstation
CALL: 0800 294 5678

MISCO.co.uk

SKYROOM OFFER

SEE, SHARE, AND SHOW YOUR WORK... ACROSS TOWN OR ACROSS THE WORLD.

HP SkyRoom is your boarding pass to super-fast, real-time, visual collaboration direct from your desktop. Combining seamless high-fi audio, HD capable[2] video and high-performance 3D application sharing, HP SkyRoom allows you to interact live with up to three others in your own virtual meeting space within your corporate network - all from the comfort of your own workspace.

Instant collaboration
Skip the travel and its toll.

- See and work visually for a face-to-face meeting experience that feels natural and in-person with a collaboration experience so seamless, fast, and smooth, it's almost like being there.
- Share live audio, video, applications, and streaming media - such as 3D engineering models or feature film dailies - through your PC, with your colleagues across the globe.
- Speed decision making while avoiding the cost and environmental impact of business travel.

Professional quality
Enjoy a virtual reality meeting experience that is as good as live.

- High-resolution capabilities make lag time, jerky video, and poor sound quality a memory.
- Imagine communicating live over your network with sub-100 millisecond latency.[3]
- Two embedded HP-designed media engines allow you to share 3D and rich media content at 15 frames per second or greater and simultaneously interact with your colleagues via video conference - without sacrificing quality.
- Keep your meeting and data more secure with AES256 advanced encryption.
- Use a VPN connection when outside your corporate network to connect and collaborate with colleagues in remote locations.

Affordable simplicity
Engineered for ease-of-use at an affordable price.

- Get to work fast with a user interface and features that make collaboration simple, intuitive, and easy to manage.
- Combining business-class performance with a consumer price, HP SkyRoom puts the power of a highly advanced visual collaboration solution within reach.
- Transform the way you work. Foster teamwork and speed decision-making while reducing your carbon footprint.

(intel) Xeon inside

Powerful. Intelligent.

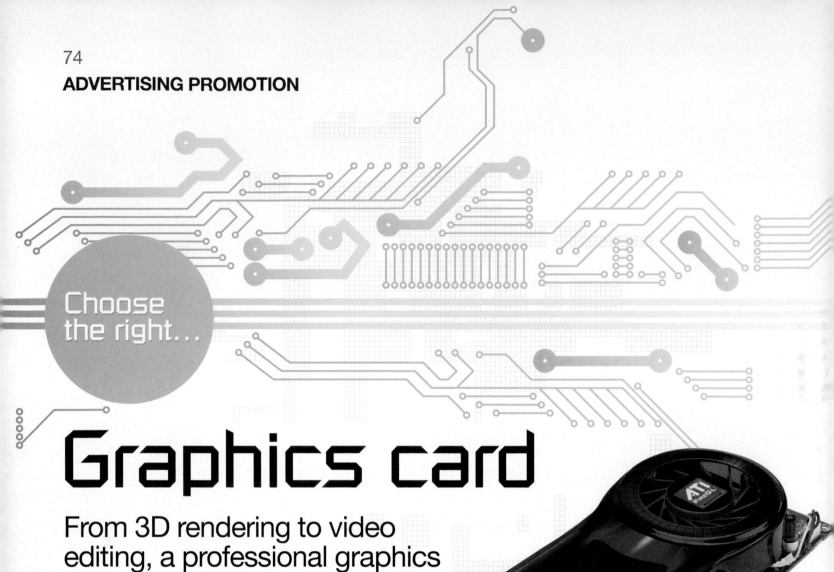

Choose the right...

Graphics card

From 3D rendering to video editing, a professional graphics card will power you through

While Photoshop, Painter and other digital painting and design applications benefit from extra RAM and CPU power, a top-spec graphics card is recommended for 3D artists and video editors. Traditionally, this market has been a two-horse race between Nvidia and ATI. Nvidia's Quadro FX series and ATI's FirePro series each support a subset of OpenGL commands for hardware acceleration, speeding particular shading and rendering tasks.

Nvidia's Quadro range was designed with some of CS4's primary functions in mind. After Effects and Premiere both benefit from the Quadro series' multithreading, enables multiple tasks to be performed at once and cutting editing and rendering time.

Nvidia's Quadro FX series cards support CUDA, which is Nvidia's answer to Stream Computing. AMD's new ATI FireGLs and FirePro take a broadly similar approach to Nvidia's Quadros, with 320 general-purpose processing units. They are therefore similarly ideal for computer-intensive tasks like rendering and video editing.

For 3D specialists, real-time 3D may be the primary motive in any purchase decision, but GPU acceleration for the final rendering stage and physics simulation are also professional touches. CUDA, for example, supports rendering plug-ins that can take advantage of cards' power.

At the opposite end of the scale, there are consumer, gamer-orientated cards such as ATI's FireGL and Nvidia's GeForce series. These offer shader modelling and GPU acceleration, and while they may not pack as much of a punch as professionally aimed cards, they're certainly more than adequate for all but the most complex 3D renders. ∎

Three of the best... graphics cards
The GPUs you need to take notice of...

What: Nvidia Quadro FX5800, from £2,791
Why: 4GB GPU, 512-bit interface, Shader Model 4.0, OpenGL 3.1, 3D Vision, SLI Support
Where: www.nvidia.com

What: ATI FirePro V5700, from £361.78
Why: 512MB GPU, Shader Model 4.1, OpenGL 3.0
Where: www.amd.com

What: Nvidia GeForce GTX 285 for Mac, from £369.95
Why: 1GB GPU, Nvidia PureVideo HD technology, OpenGL optimisation
Where: www.nvidia.com

Ultra performance, bargain price.

Five star* winning professional graphics card at £500 now only £179! **

Discover the pixel-perfect accelerator
for your application at:
www.amd.com/firepro/

Sale!
ATI FireGL™ V7700
Up to £300 off!

For a limited period.

£179**

ATI FirePro™ Graphics Accelerators. No Boundaries.

ATI FirePro™ from AMD destroys previous benchmarks to deliver the premium performance you need to explore new territory with your 3D applications.

The ATI FireGL™ V7700 supports 10 bit in photoshop ***, fully certified for most applications with add in drivers and driver tuning for the applications you use.

Why wait? Create now!

ATI FireGL™ V7700

Workstation Specialists
Call. +44 (0) 800 180 480

workstationspecialists.com

Xworks
Call. +44 (0) 1785 229 191

xworksinteractive.com

Armari
Call. +44 (0) 1923 225 550

www.armari.com

Scan
Call. +44 (0) 8714 724 747

www.scan.co.uk

AMD
The future is fusion

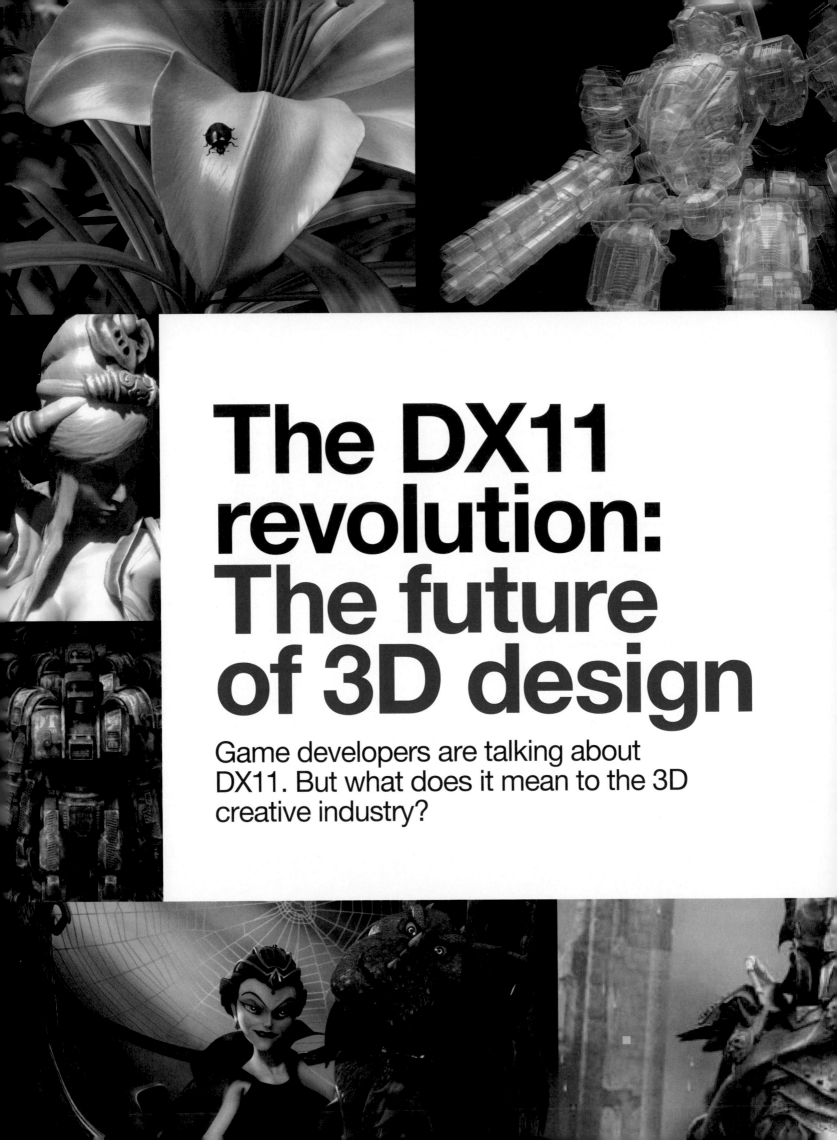

The DX11 revolution: The future of 3D design

Game developers are talking about DX11. But what does it mean to the 3D creative industry?

With the release of Direct X11, 3D artists and designers can make use of powerful new accelerated hardware and software in their creation process.

Direct X is currently used by several 3D creative applications as a 3D engine, including 3ds Max – a program heavily used in games design and development. Currently, the 3ds Max engine is based on DX9, with elements of DX10 used in its shaders to provide lighting effects. Like other creative applications, though, 3ds Max also supports multithreading.

The new Direct X11 API introduces improved multithreading processes, and can now handle elements such as display lists with ease. Display lists refer to graphics card GPU data that is passed backwards and forwards between the computer's system memory. By using multiple cores, the CPU remains unobstructed by this data, enabling software tasks to be carried out quickly and efficiently, with an average speed increase of between 20 and 50 per cent.

DX11 also offers new compute shaders, which can handle post processing including physics, AI and particle systems. Most 3D animation software supports these features, and uses CPU or GPU to handle such tasks. DX11 has improved access to the geometry to do the operations itself, so is far faster than existing methods.

"At the moment, post-processing is done using pixel shaders and it can be quite hard to get the efficiency out of the hardware," says Richard Huddy, ISV development manager at AMD. "We think compute shaders are going to give significant performance [enhancement] in that specific area of code."

Tessellation: when performance meets quality

Tessellation is a way of transforming data in one form to another on the fly, and can generate highly detailed objects using fewer resources than traditional technology.

Tessellation takes existing meshes and enhances certain sections of the model to give more detail. It can also be used as a method of reducing detail in a scene, in order to increase speed. ATI graphics cards have had this feature for several generations now, including the FirePro series, while the Xenos graphics chip in the Xbox 360 also supports this capability.

3ds Max uses .fx shaders to show depth of field and motion blur that can be taken to the final render, and here DX11 enhances the processes. StudioGPU's software MachStudio Pro already sports some of these capabilities in a rasterizer format, while roughly 85 per cent of applications use a rasterizer approach, including most 3D creation applications.

With the DX11 hardware already out, this gives a new level of performance, plus features to enable functions such as real-time raytracing that have a effect on the day-to-day production of 3D. New features such Eyefinity – where up to six screens can be driven from one GPU – is changing the face of 3D design.

Having one GPU driving six screens prevents sync problems associated with linking up multiple GPUs. This reduces the cost from tens of thousands to thousands, making this technology easily accessible.

With exciting new technologies like DX11 on the horizon, the face of 3D art, illustration, video work and design is set to change forever.

Choose
the right…

Monitor

When choosing a monitor, it pays dividends to go for the biggest and best your budget will stretch to

The dramatic price difference between mid-market and high-end monitors is easily explained. One key factor is colour accuracy. On cheaper monitors, any change in brightness will change the colour accuracy, while on a high-end model you can change one without changing the other. Gamut – the visible range of colours that a monitor can display – is a huge factor in motion graphics work and photographic design, as motion graphics and cinema monitors need to be able to display a gamut called the NTSC standard. This is critical if you're grading live-action or 3D animations, because if the gamut is limited you won't be able to see what you're doing, and you won't get the end results you're expecting.

Design is yet another factor, as the trade-off is between looks and ergonomics. The box-on-a-stick solution is popular because it's easily adjustable. You need to be able to set the height of a monitor so that it's at eye level, and the tilt so that you're viewing it face on. This isn't just about comfort – brightness and colour can shift as you move away from the ideal viewing position.

Newer monitors combine LED backlighting with a traditional LCD panel, using a grid of LEDs instead of a plastic light panel. This can't compensate for a poor viewing angle on the LCD panel but does create a much smoother backlight that stays bright across a wider angle. Affordable LED backlighting and panels with wider gamut and viewing angles are moving into the mid-market, making them a realistic choice for creative needs. ∎

Three of the best… monitors
The displays you should look out for

What: BenQ v2400Eco, £199
Why: 1920x1080 resolution, 24-inch, 5ms pixel response rate, 1000:1 contrast ratio DSUB/HDMI, LED backlight
Where: www.benq.co.uk

What: Samsung XL2370, £300
Why: 1920x1080, 22-inch, 2ms pixel response rate, 1000:1 contrast ratio, HDMI, DVI-D/HDCP compliant, LED backlight
Where: www.samsung.com/uk

What: NEC MultiSync EA222WMe, £316.08
Why: 1680x1050, 22-inch, 30,000 dynamic contrast ratio VGA, DVI, USB and DisplayPort, 6:10 widescreen display with W-LED backlight
Where: www.nec-display-solutions.co.uk

Choose the right...

Digital SLR

Capture images like a pro with our DSLR guide

Affordable digital cameras have eliminated the inconvenience, risk and drudgery of light room processing, making it possible for anyone to take good photos for professional creative use.More isn't always better, however, especially when it comes to megapixels. Digital camera designers have to trade noise against resolution so, without extra sensitivity and digital processing, more megapixels may mean more noise rather than more detail.

In terms of camera hardware, budget super-zooms offer excellent value for money. With prices from £150, they offer most of the image quality and features of mid-market SLRs in a portable form so, if your output is primarily for web or product shots, you don't need to spend a fortune. Mid-market super-zooms offer impressive telephoto to macro (close-up) capabilities, but do make sure you buy a model with RAW mode – a 'digital negative' straight from the CCD – for the best image quality.

The primary strength of an SLR is the ability to swap its lenses. Good lenses are pin-sharp and offer apertures down to F2.8, which means they'll capture the available light more successfully than those limited to higher F-stop numbers. A full SLR kit needs a selection of lenses and, with prices ranging from £200 to £1000 for each lens, the costs can soon mount up. ■

Three of the best... digital SLRs
The cameras to look out for

What: Fuji FinePix S100FS, £499
Why: 11m pixel Super CCD HR VIII, 2.5inch tilting LCD monitor, 14.3x Fujinon manual zoom lens
Where: www.fujifilm.co.uk

What: Nikon D60 10MP, £350
Why: 18-55mm zoom lens, 10.2 megapixel CCD sensor, TTL full-aperture exposure metering system
Where: www.nikon.co.uk

What: Canon EOS 1DS Mk III, £4,670
Why: 21 megapixel full-frame CMOS sensor, five frames-per-second shooting, ISO 100-1600, auto focus system with 19 cross type sensors and 26 focus assist points
Where: www.canon.co.uk

Choose the right...

Printer

A decent printer is essential to any creative pro. Here's what to look for

A good quality printer is an important asset in any digital creative's studio. But, due to the diversity of the different outputted material, there's no one-size-fits-all solution. The market is dominated by photo printers because they offer the most accurate colour output with the widest gamut. The catch is the running cost – for smaller printers, a full set of inks can set you back around half as much as the printer itself. So, the key is to do your homework on how much replacement inks will be.

Size is also something you'll need to consider. A3 is a good compromise format; it's a realistic maximum proof size for a smaller studio, but it can also print smaller sizes down to A6. At the A3 and smaller end of the market, most models support third-party inks – which can save as much as 50 per cent on the cost of a full ink set.

The main manufacturers – Canon, Epson and HP – have crafted different but related ink technologies. Canon arguably leads the way with its 12-ink Lucia system, which gives a very wide printed gamut and means you can swap out cartridges less frequently. Epson's K3 UltraChrome format uses eight inks, including two black cartridges – one for gloss and one for matte media. HP's Vivera system, meanwhile, uses eight inks for wide gamut colour that's comparable with the competition, with the disadvantage of relatively limited life.

It's worth investigating the longevity of a printer's output. Expect some visible fading within a couple of years on unlaminated stock, and investigate how long inks can expect to stay bright for, as fading may be an issue for collectable prints or commercial art. ∎

Three of the best... printers
Make sure the output is as good as the idea

What: Epson Stylus R2880, £655.73 (incl. VAT)
Why: A3+ sizing, 4800 optimised dpi, eight-colour K3 pigment inks
Where: www.epson.co.uk

What: HP B8850, £399
Why: A3+ sizing, 4800 optimised dpi, eight-colour Vivera pigment inks (including two blacks)
Where: www.hp.com

What: Canon Pixma Pro, £542.97
Why: A3+ sizing, 4800 dpi, 10 colour, PictBridge technology
Where: www.canon.co.uk

Choose the right…

Camcorder

Reduce time and effort in post-production with a camera that delivers quality footage from the word go…

For creative video professionals, capturing the highest quality footage is of primary importance. Fixing problems in post-production is one thing, but when it comes to capturing raw footage you want to record at the highest available resolution. Ultimately, this means using an HD camcorder.

So how much better is HD than SD? SD PAL is 720x576 at 25 frames per second (fps), so there's a big difference in quality and resolution compared to even the basic HD resolution of 720p, which records at 1280x720, 50fps. Uncompressed HD 720p uses roughly four times the bandwidth of SD, which means HD takes up more disk space and also needs much faster disks – so bear this in mind when pairing your camcorder with your workstation.

Portability is definitely another key consideration, together with cost. The more professional your camcorder, the heavier and more unwieldy kit tends to become. But the payoff is in quality of recording, which stretches to sound too; if you opt for a cheaper mid-market camcorder, chances are that you'll need an external mic to capture sound at sufficient quality.

As ever, choosing the right kit for your needs comes down to a balance of price, portability and requirements. For web video and raw footage, a mid-market HD camcorder is more than capable, but for anything more professional it pays dividends to buy the best kit you can afford. ∎

Three of the best… camcorders
HD offerings of the moment

What: Sony HDR-SR10, £629
Why: 1920x1080i high definition video, image stabiliser, Dolby digital sound, MPEG-4 AVC/H.264, 40GB SR10 memory
Where: www.sonybiz.net

What: Panasonic HDC-SD200, £499
Why: Full HD 1920x1080, 3MOS camcorder system, intelligent auto mode and AF tracking, 1.6 lux low-light recording
Where: www.panasonic.co.uk

What: Canon XH A1s, £3,039
Why: 1080i HD capture, 20x lens with separate focus, zoom and iris rings, HD-SDI with embedded audio, optional NTSC upgrade
Where: www.canon-europe.com

professional, every time

SmartFlash 200

The new top value studio flash kit from Lencarta that's streets ahead

Guide No. 100 @ 100 ISO
Stepless adjustment over 4 stops
Powerful 250w modelling lamp
Ultra fast recycling
Fully compatible with all Bowens fit accessories
Super efficient fan cooling

Complete kits from under £250
Top quality at bottom prices!

www.lencarta.com
0845 618 2889

Have you cracked the cover code?

US and Rest of World readers: Your cover was different to the UK and subscribers' cover, so the artwork is above. Can you crack the code?

On the disc
Looking for the files
needed to complete one
of our tutorials? Don't
worry – you'll find them
all on your free CD

Technique

Learn new software skills and creative techniques with our inspirational tutorial guides – all written by the industry's leading creative professionals

**Create type
with flair** 86
Tom Lane's masterclass
in illustrative type

**Multi-platform
characters** 90
Create characters for a
range of ad mediums

**Create Flash
photo mosaics** 94
Build photo mosaic
art via your webcam

**Inspiration
Workshop** 98
Spiral Studio explains its
haunting artworks

102 **Table tips
in InDesign**
Jo Gulliver brings
simplicity to the table

103 **From Illustrator
to Flash**
Tips and tricks to move
smoothly through Flash

104 **Explosive
animation**
Alex Donne Johnson
shares his incredible
motion technique

108 **Brief Encounter**
Nick Scott Studio
celebrates Google's life

112 **Make abstract
communicate**
Gordon Reid shows you
how to clear the way in
abstract design

Ads with character _Page 90

Creating Photoshop typography with flair _Page 86

The life of Google in a new short _Page 108

Explosive 3D animation techniques _Page 104

Spiral Studio's fairytale figures _Page 98

Communicate with abstract design _Page 112

Photoshop and Illustrator CS3 or later

Build type with flair

Who says type has to be plain to be bold? **Tom Lane** demonstrates how to draw on pattern work to add intricate detail to your type designs

For years I've drawn inspiration from the artwork of ancient cultures. Back in 2002, whilst at university studying graphic design, I discovered some beautiful examples of ancient Greek pattern work, and from that point I was hooked. I had never spent much time trying to draw anything with such intricacy before, and at that time I certainly didn't know Adobe Illustrator very well.

In the years proceeding, I learnt to draw the patterns accurately and built up my confidence until I was able to express myself with the skills I had developed. Which leads me nicely to this tutorial. I've sketched out some elements for you to redraw in Illustrator, and these elements will be used to embellish the typographic element I have supplied on the disc and set the composition of the piece. We'll then move into Photoshop where we'll add texture, colour and adjustment layers to give it that extra zing. Let's go!

Tom Lane
__ The multi-disciplined, fiery headed gent at the helm of Ginger Monkey, devises exquisite and inspirational designs for an international client list that includes Sony Ericsson, Coca-Cola, Miller Beer and Mercedes-Benz. To see more of his work go to www.ginger monkeydesign.com

On the disc
The files accompanying this tutorial can be located in DiscContents\ Resources\ Embellish

Time needed
10 hours

Skills
___ Drawing in Illustrator
___ Using the Pathfinder palette
___ Texturing elements in Photoshop
___ Colouring in Photoshop
___ Using adjustment layers

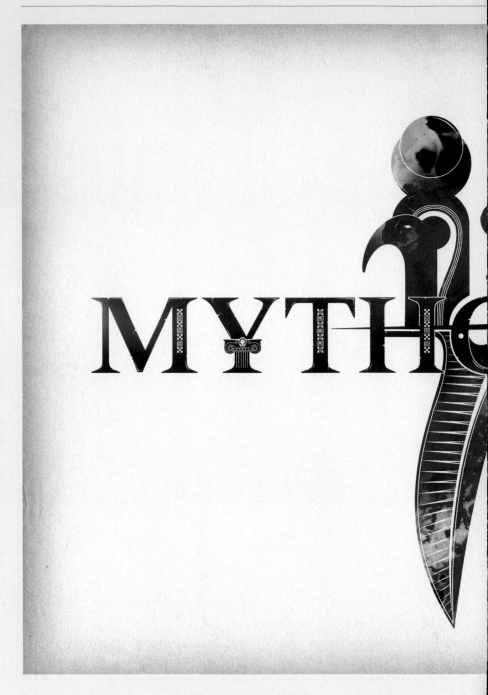

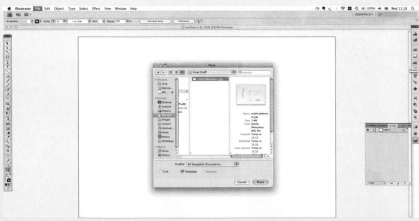

01_____ In Illustrator, create a new A3 landscape document. Go to File>Place and select the file mythicalelement.jpg from the disc. Before you select 'Place', check the 'Template' box at the bottom left of the dialog box.

04_____Once the solid shapes are set, begin to add the detail on top with white strokes and filled objects. We need to switch the colours between no fill and black/white fill in the toolbar so we can see what's below and make adjustments. This will become second nature after a while.

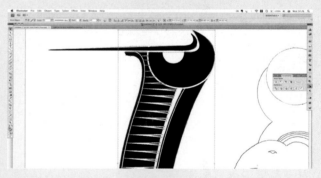

05_____When that's complete, make a copy of the wing and paste to the side of your Artboard. Open the Pathfinder palette. Select all the white solid shapes and the black solid shape below, and click Subtract on the Pathfinder palette. Click Object>Expand and check the Stroke box before subtracting in the Pathfinder palette.

02_____For this particular piece we want solid surfaces we can add texture to later in Photoshop, so we're going to draw the elements predominantly in black with white for detail. Select the Pen tool and choose a black fill from the toolbar.

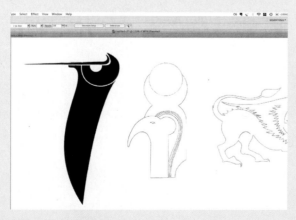

03_____Begin to trace the wing shape to make it solid with black. Really focus on trying to make the lines flow with as few anchor points as possible. This will help create smoother lines.

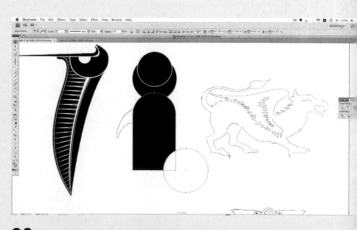

06_____Select all the objects forming the wing and click 'Add' in the Pathfinder palette. For the next object we can use the Shape tool as well as the Pen tool to help build the structure. Again, use the Pathfinder palette to help build the objects. →

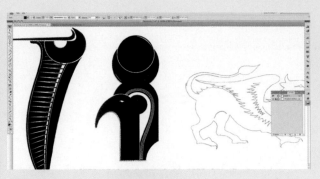

07 When you've drawn all the elements, give the ibis head a 2pt white stroke line around both the circle at the top and the shape that makes up the nose, ear and neck. The latter needs to be on top of everything except the eye. Select Object>Arrange and bring the objects forward or backward.

08 Now we repeat Step 5 to finish the ibis head, so we're left with a single object. Next, we move on to the griffin. Begin by drawing the basic outline as solid black with the Pen tool. Add the extra details (such as the spines on the griffin's back) one at a time, then add the white detail.

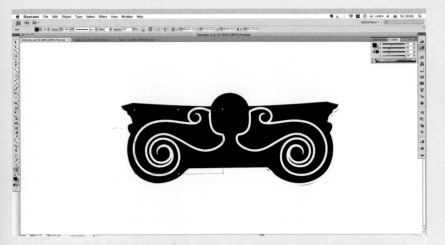

09 Repeat Step 5 to turn the griffin into a single element. Now it's time to move onto the pillar. Use the same techniques you've developed over the last few steps to build this element. Make sure to turn it into a single element once complete.

10 Now open the file Mythologytext.eps from the disc. Start by copying and pasting the wing element behind the 'O' in the middle. You'll need to adjust the size to fit; simply hold Shift and drag the corners of the bounding box to scale. Then add the head and the griffin.

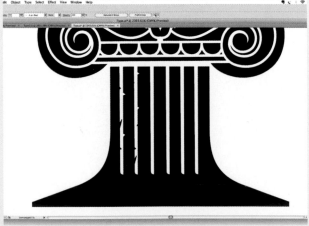

11 Now add the pillars to the two Ys and the L. You'll need to add some extra white shapes behind the pillar element to separate it from the character. Use the Pathfinder palette to subtract these new shapes from the character below. Refer to the Stroke palette once done, and select 'Align Stroke Outside'.

12 It's time to add some details to the type. Begin by creating the lines for the pillars. Use the Rectangle tool to draw the vertical lines. Then, with the Pen tool, add little triangle 'nicks' and 'spikes' in black and white.

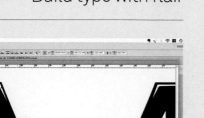

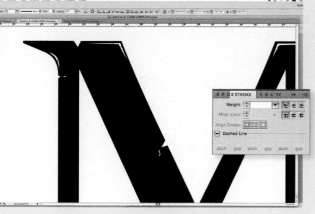

13_____ Apply this technique to distress the rest of the characters. I've supplied some smaller details as sketches on the disc, which you can use to add finishing touches. Be sure to 'Subtract' and 'Add' using the Pathfinder palette as you go.

14_____ If you feel comfortable using the Pathfinder palette, begin turning the whole illustration into a single element by subtracting and adding elements. If not, copy and paste all the objects together into a new A3 landscape document in Photoshop. Go to Select>Colour Range and use the Eyedropper tool to select the black. Hit OK.

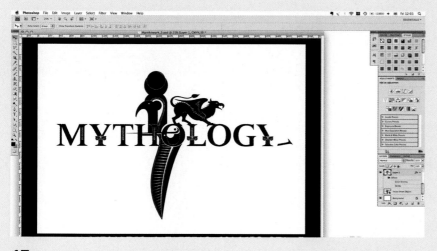

15_____ A marquee should now be visible. On a new layer we hit Shift+Delete and fill this with black. We turn off the original layer below, and we're left with just the black fill of our illustration. Open the file painttexture.tiff from the disc, copy it and paste it twice into the document.

16_____ Hide one of the paint textures and position the other over the ibis head and the griffin. Hover the cursor over the layer thumbnail in the Layers palette, holding Ctrl/Cmd. Click the thumbnail and a marquee should appear. Select>Inverse> Delete. Repeat for the second paint layer to cover the wing.

17_____ Now double-click your lower illustration layer and select an orange colour overlay. Set the opacity to 17%. Select the texture layer covering the wing, and select the third icon from the left (Add Vector Mask). Use a black-to-no-fill gradient to mask the edges of the image.

18_____ Hover your cursor over the layer thumbnail of your lowest illustration layer and click whilst holding Ctrl/Cmd. On a new layer and within this selection, use the Gradient tool to darken areas of the illustration. Finally, use the Hue, Colour Balance and Levels adjustment layers to bring the colours closer together.

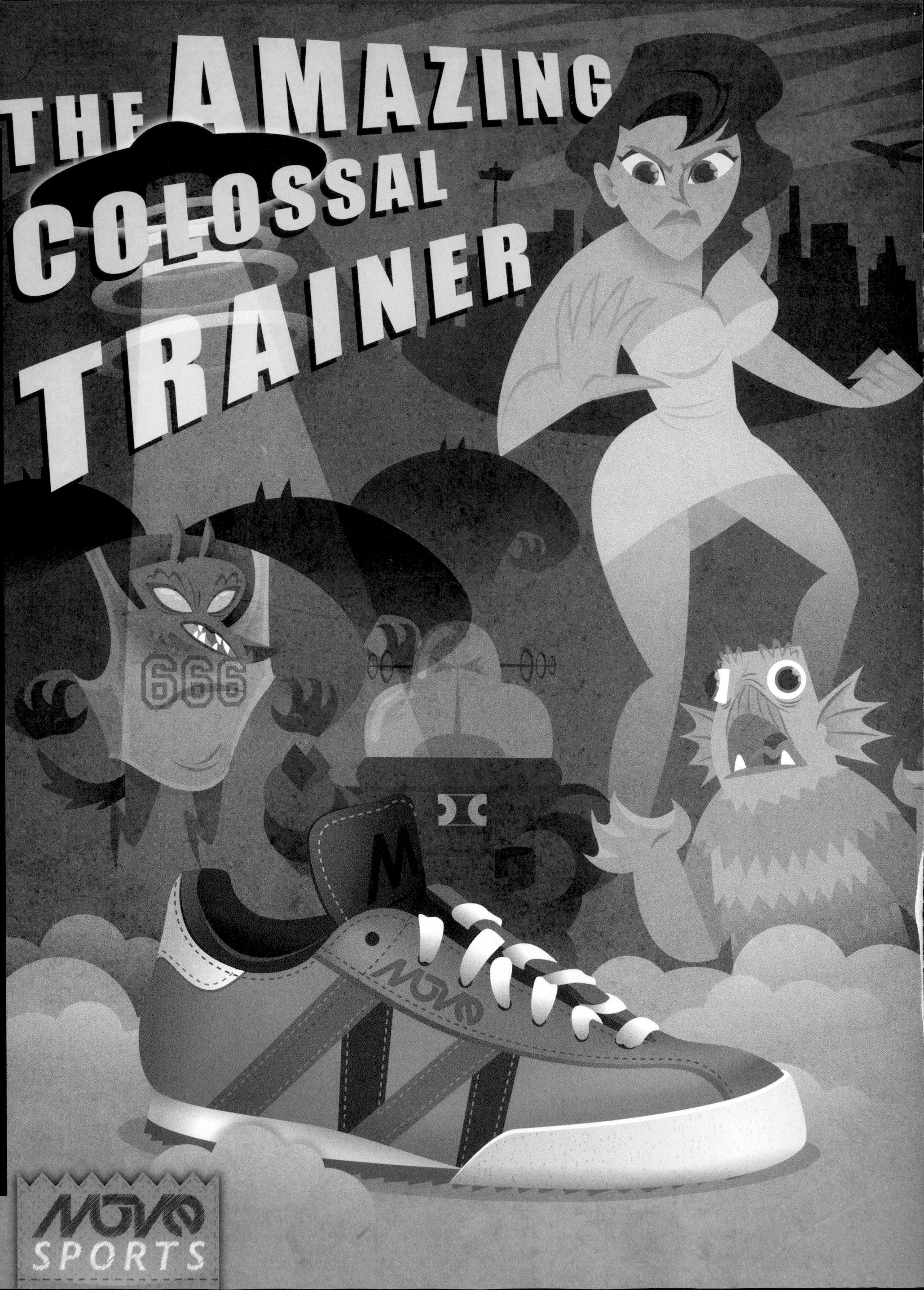
THE AMAZING COLOSSAL TRAINER
666
M
MOVE
MOVE SPORTS

Illustrator CS2 and later

Cross-platform character design

Ben Mounsey shows you how to create characters that are easily transferable across the range of modern ad display mediums

Creative, striking ad campaigns are what sell brands and stick in minds, and success in producing such output is worth its weight in gold. A campaign for a product can be diverse in its range of applications; a client wanting to use the core elements you've created in several different formats, from various print dimensions to web, is nothing out of the ordinary. In this tutorial I'll be taking you through steps to create a versatile design in Illustrator, taking your core design elements from a magazine-style layout to a web banner. Illustrator is the perfect tool for this, as with its multiple artboards it enables us to work with our design across several formats.

Ben Mounsey
__ Also known as 'green glasses', Ben Mounsey lives in London, working freelance in the animation and illustration industries. His client list includes the likes of Cartoon Network and Nickelodeon, and showcased in his work is a love of '50s retro, humour, big characters and hats. See www. greenglasses.co.uk

On the disc
The files accompanying this tutorial can be located in DiscContents\ Resources\ Illustrator

Time needed
4-5 hours

Skills
—— Using clipping masks
—— Using Pathfinder tools
—— Handling textures in Illustrator
—— Using multiple artboards
—— Using Warp effects on text

01____It wasn't difficult for me to choose a theme, as drawing on inspiration from '50s icons is always sure to spark my imagination. Once you've sourced your visual inspiration, grab the sketchbook. Sketch out your ideas on paper first to get a rough composition.

02____Next I work on my characters. I pick a few memorable '50s sci-fi icons: Robby the Robot, a werewolf, the Creature from the Black Lagoon, a flying saucer and a 50-foot woman. I sketch out the basic design of each character (this can be found in Characters.ai on the disc). The flying saucer is completed, as an example.

03____Now to artwork the characters. I like to break my designs into basic shapes, creating nice a balance of hard edges and curves – the Pen tool's Bézier curves are perfect for this. Flesh out your characters with expression lines, and work in greyscale to really make your product 'pop'! For colour reference, check the Final.ai file.

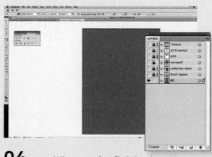

04____When you've finished your characters, copy and paste them into your Starter.ai file, which you'll find on the disc. Distribute them to layers and hide them. Add a new blank layer at the bottom – this will be our backdrop. Use the Rectangle tool to make a new grey (#6E6D70) rectangle the size of our page. And try to keep organised by naming your layers!

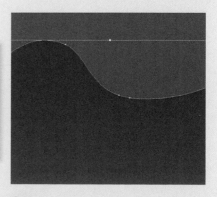

05____Copy another rectangle and paste in front (Ctrl/Cmd+F). Take the Knife tool and make a pleasing curve for the backdrop (this should look like a hill). Delete the top half and make the bottom half a vertical black-to-transparent gradient. →

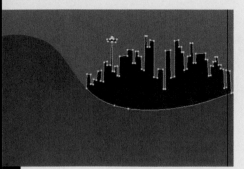

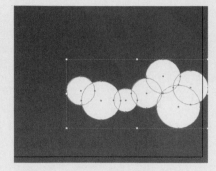

06_____ Use the Pen tool to rough out a freehand blocky cityscape in a slightly darker grey. Don't worry about being too precise. Take the curve gradient, copy and paste it in front of the cityscape, and with both elements selected use the Minus Front command in the Pathfinder palette to create a seamless cut.

07_____ For filmic ambience, we'll draw some eerie mist. On a new layer, use the Ellipse tool and hold down Shift to draw some fixed ratio circles. Select a very light grey colour. Once you've covered the lower half of the image, select the circles and select Unite from the Pathfinder palette. Set the opacity for the new shape to around 60%.

08_____ Turn on your character layers and arrange them behind the mist layer. You can use a background colour grey-to-transparent gradient shape to blend your characters' lower halves into the scene. Scale and shift your characters about until they sit well.

09_____ Now we're going to crowd the scene with a pack of werewolves! Select the werewolf character, copy and paste him, then use the Pathfinder palette's Unite tool to combine him into one solid shape. Make the clone a vertical black-to-transparent gradient. Duplicate your clone a few times.

Tracing tip
When tracing artwork, move the sketch layer to be above and set it to Multiply in the Transparency palette. This helps you to see what you're doing more clearly.

10_____ Now to add the text. I've come up with a twist on the movie title *The Amazing Colossal Man*. Choose Impact as a font and play with the word sizes for a dynamic look. Make it a striking yellow, then go to Effect>Warp>Arc apply an arc styling. Expand the text, copy it, paste the copy behind and offset this copy slightly, giving it a black fill.

Visual CV
In pictures: a guide to the career and work of our Technique writers

Ben Mounsey
The Green Glasses man selects five favourite past projects

Skatoony Three-Headed Monster – July 2007
A character design sheet for *Skatoony*, a series created by Cartoon Network.

'Bus Stop' – February 2009
A self-promotional piece used for business cards and mailouts. It's part of a series of my images in which I explore texture in my work.

11_____ Turn on the layer named Texture1, which will cover your page. Select it and, in the Transparency panel, set it to Soft Light with an opacity of 80%. This should marry the texture with the artwork, resulting in an aged look to the piece and adding some subtle hues to the greyscale elements.

12_____ Now open the file Product_brand.ai from the disc, copy the logo and trainer elements, and paste them to layers above the texture. Nest the trainer in with the mist by adding some extra fluff to the mist by repeating Step 7. Use a white-to-transparent gradient to blend.

13_____ In order to sit the trainer in with the mist, I've created a clipping mask. Select some of your 'mist fluff', sit it slightly in front of the shoe, and copy it. Using the Pen tool, draw a solid shape that blacks out the shoe, then paste the 'mist fluff' in front. Select both the fluff and the black shape and use the Minus Front tool in the Pathfinder palette. Select that new shape and the shoe behind it, and go to Object>Clipping Mask>Make.

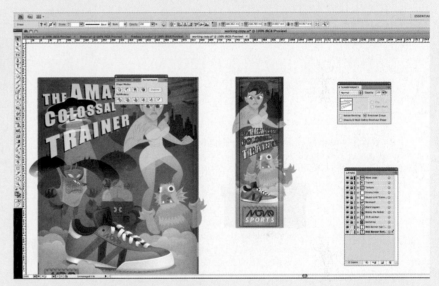

14_____ By now you should have your finished composition. To use our elements for a new composition, we'll need to create a new artboard. Select the Artboard tool (Shift+O) and drag a new square (don't worry about the dimensions), then go to the top bar and enter a width of 160px and a height of 600px (a standard 'sky scraper' web banner). Hit Enter.

15_____ With your new artboard set up, simply copy across the elements you want in your new composition using the styling principles we've already run through. Note that when scaling objects using the Scale tool, have 'Scale Strokes & Effects' turned on to keep your quality of line. You can find my design in the Final.ai file.

Walls/Unilever character designs – March 2009
Character designs for a campaign for Walls ice cream. The brief was to come up with trendy, cool characters that kids would identify with.

'Alice in Wonderland' promo piece – August 2009
A promotional piece for my agent, The Organisation, earlier this year, the theme was to depict an image from the world of *Alice in Wonderland*.

'Banjo Bliss' – September 2009
A self-initiated piece to explore the use of line in my artwork. It also showcases my love of folk music.

Flash CS4, ActionScript 3

Create photo mosaics with your webcam

Matt Booth

demonstrates how to build photo mosaic masterpieces via nifty webcam and Flash skills

With the help of your webcam and a few photographs, it's easy to create striking photographic mosaic representations of what is displayed through the webcam. In this tutorial I'll show you how to import your photographs via XML, and get an average colour and brightness for each photograph. Then, using this information, we will work out the average colour and brightness of the pixels from the webcam, and place the correct colour image in its place. To achieve a movie with more depth, you just need to use more photos; the wider the range of colours and brightness, the better. You'll find the screen grabs for each step of this tutorial in full on this issue's disc.

Matt Booth
__ Booth is a digital creative who has worked with agencies such as Poke, Domani Studios and McFaul and for brands such as Red Bull, Calypso and Hudson Jeans. His folio can be viewed at www.flashtemple.com

On the disc
The files accompanying this tutorial can be located in DiscContents\Resources\Mosaic

Time needed
1 hour

Skills
__ ActionScript 3
__ Dynamic loading of external XML and images
__ Working out average pixel colour and brightness

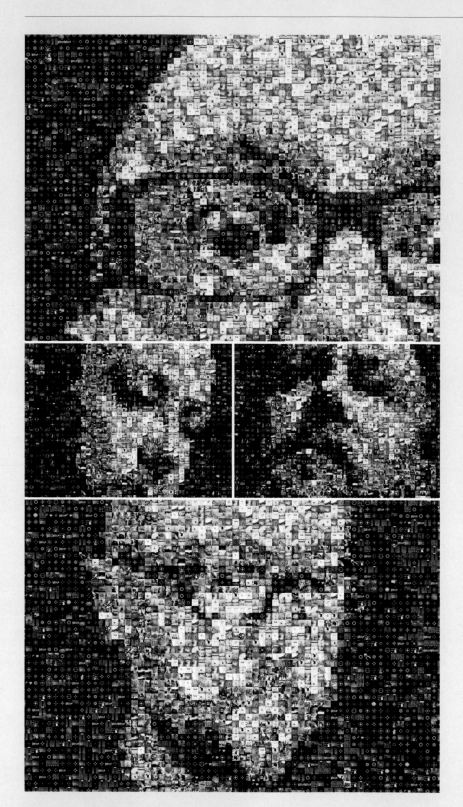

01____ The first step is to get your images ready. The images in this tutorial are 75x75px. We will only be using them at 16x16px, but it's good to have the option to use them bigger. The more images you use, the better. We are using 450 images here. Also use a wide range of coloured and dark/light images. Once you have your images ready, place them in a folder and call it 'images'.

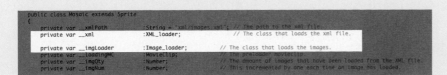

```
public class Mosaic extends Sprite
{
    private var __xmlPath        :String = "xml/images.xml"; // The path to the xml file.
    private var __xml            :XML_loader;               // The class that loads the xml file.

    private var __imgLoader      :Image_loader;             // The class that loads the images.
    private var __loadingMC       :MovieClip;                // The preloader movieclip.
    private var __imgQty          :Number;                   // The amount of images that have been loaded from the XML file.
    private var __imgNum          :Number;                   // This incremented by one each time an image has loaded.
```

02_____ Now to explain our three main classes, which you will find in the 'com' folder on the disc: XML_loader.as loads the XML file; Image_loader.as loads in all the images specified in the XML file; mosaic.as brings the two other classes together, starts the webcam, does all the colour calculations and displays the mosaic. It's this class that we will concentrate on.

```
public class Mosaic extends Sprite
{
    private var __xmlPath        :String = "xml/images.xml"; // The path to the xml file.
    private var __xml            :XML_loader;               // The class that loads the xml file.

    private var __imgLoader      :Image_loader;             // The class that loads the images.
    private var __loadingMC       :MovieClip;                // The preloader movieclip.
    private var __imgQty          :Number;                   // The amount of images that have been loaded from the XML file.
    private var __imgNum          :Number;                   // This incremented by one each time an image has loaded.

    private var __arrRedDark     :Array = new Array();       // The dark red array of images.
    private var __arrRedMid      :Array = new Array();       // The mid red array of images.
    private var __arrRedLight    :Array = new Array();       // The light red array of images.

    private var __arrGreenDark   :Array = new Array();       // The dark green array of images.
    private var __arrGreenMid    :Array = new Array();       // The mid green array of images.
    private var __arrGreenLight  :Array = new Array();       // The light green array of images.

    private var __arrBlueDark    :Array = new Array();       // The dark blue array of images.
    private var __arrBlueMid     :Array = new Array();       // The mid blue array of images.
    private var __arrBlueLight   :Array = new Array();       // The light blue array of images.

    private var __arrGreyDark    :Array = new Array();       // The dark grey array of images.
    private var __arrGreyMid     :Array = new Array();       // The mid grey array of images.
    private var __arrGreyLight   :Array = new Array();       // The light grey array of images.

    private var __pixelSize      :Number = 16;               // The size of the mosaic pixels.

    private var __cameraWidth    :Number = 640;              // The width of the camera.
    private var __cameraHeight   :Number = 480;              // The height of the camera.

    private var __videoBitmapData :BitmapData = new BitmapData( __cameraWidth, __cameraHeight, false, 0xFFFFFF ); // The bitmap data of the webcam.

    private var __camera         :Camera;                    // The webcam object.
    private var __video          :Video;                     // The video object.
```

03_____ Firstly all the variables are declared. These include the path to the XML file, the image loader class, the arrays for storing the BitmapData of the imported images (depending on their average colour and brightness), the pixel size of the mosaic, the camera dimensions, and camera and video objects.

```
images.xml

<?xml version="1.0" encoding="UTF-8"?>
<images>
    <img>images/2827075343_44ec17734d_s.jpg</img>
    <img>images/2827076871_15b944c708_s.jpg</img>
    <img>images/2827077487_a6031ef7f9_s.jpg</img>
    <img>images/2827080731_50472ac27f_s.jpg</img>
    <img>images/2827083511_9b33e8668b_s.jpg</img>
    <img>images/2827084801_35bd155880_s.jpg</img>
    <img>images/2827085453_3f636c17f1_s.jpg</img>
    <img>images/2827093713_55db1067ea_s.jpg</img>
    <img>images/2827094365_2b1a227d8a_s.jpg</img>
    <img>images/2827095081_3bacca4262_s.jpg</img>
    <img>images/2827099401_f054b4ece8_s.jpg</img>
    <img>images/2827100073_091342ae4f_s.jpg</img>
    <img>images/2827319131_b69cc6f224_s.jpg</img>
    <img>images/2827319555_d94a4f5d72_s.jpg</img>
    <img>images/2827912812_e1a937a6aa_s.jpg</img>
    <img>images/2827914912_5e8fdb5b76_s.jpg</img>
    <img>images/2827915174_978268a858_s.jpg</img>
    <img>images/2827915984_fa7a983c8e_s.jpg</img>
    <img>images/2827916722_de897981ff_s.jpg</img>
    <img>images/2827918120_4cffd573e2_s.jpg</img>
    <img>images/2827918716_d0ed133d25_s.jpg</img>
    <img>images/2827919738_39d24367bc_s.jpg</img>
    <img>images/2827920884_976d5ff160_s.jpg</img>
    <img>images/2827929768_470195a714_s.jpg</img>
    <img>images/2827932736_13d7b83d2a_s.jpg</img>
    <img>images/2827933378_989b90246b_s.jpg</img>

Line:   4  Column:   1   XML          Tab Size:  4
```

04_____ Now we need to set up and load our XML file. In a folder called 'xml', create an XML file called images.xml and set it out with your photos, as shown. The first part of each image node is the image folder images. The next part is the name of the image along with the JPG extension.

```
private function loadXML():void
{
    // Add the preloader from the library.
    __loadingMC       = new preloader();
    __loadingMC.x     = __cameraWidth * 0.5;
    __loadingMC.y     = __cameraHeight * 0.5;

    addChild(__loadingMC);

    // Start theloading of the xml.
    __xml = new XML_loader(__xmlPath);
    initListeners(__xml, xmlLoaded, "UPDATED");
}


private function xmlLoaded(e:Event):void
{
```

05_____ Now we load the XML. Onto the stage we drop a Movie Clip from the library, which has the linkage name 'preloader'. We then add a listener to check when the XML has loaded. Then, we set the __imageQty variable with the amount of images from the XML file, and set the __imageNum variable to 0. Then, by calling the loadImages function, we start to load in each image from our images folder.

```
private function loadImages():void
{
    // Update the preloader with how many images have loaded.
    __loadingMC.txt1.text = __imgNum;
    __loadingMC.txt2.text = __imgQty;

    // Load each image.
    __imgLoader.loadImage(__xml.getXML.img[__imgNum]);
}
```

06_____ Before we can start the webcam, we need to load each image, work out if it's predominantly red, green, blue or grey and its brightness, then store it in the appropriate array (for example, __arrGreenMid). So, in the loadImages function, we update the preloader with how many images have been loaded, then we start the next image loading by the loadImage function in the Image_loader class.

<u>Keep it light</u>
Make sure you are in a well-lit room when doing this tutorial. Try connecting an external video camera instead of your built-in webcam for higher quality images. The tutorial can also be done with a Flickr feed in place of images on your computer.

```
private function imgLoaded(e:Event):void
{
    // The bitmap data of each image that has loaded.
    var bitmapData:BitmapData  = new BitmapData( 75, 75, false, 0xFFFFFF );
    var bitmap:Bitmap          = new Bitmap(bitmapData);
    bitmap.smoothing           = true;
    bitmapData.draw(__imgLoader.getBmp);

    // This function works out the average colour of each loaded image.
    averageColour(bitmapData);
```

```
private function averageColour( bmpData:BitmapData ):void
{
    // Initialise the colour variables.
    var count:Number   = 0;
    var red:Number     = 0;
    var green:Number   = 0;
    var blue:Number    = 0;

    // Work out the average colour of each image based on the width and height of the image.
    for (var x:int = 0; x < bmpData.width; x++)
    {
        for (var y:int = 0; y < bmpData.height; y++)
        {
            var pixelColour:Number = bmpData.getPixel(x, y);

            red    += getRed(pixelColour);
            green  += getGreen(pixelColour);
            blue   += getBlue(pixelColour);

            count++
        }
    }

    red   /= count;
    green /= count;
    blue  /= count;

    // Work out the brightness of each image.
    var bright:Number  = getBright(red, green, blue);
```

07_____ To work out the average colour of each loaded image, we first get the BitmapData then pass that to the averageColour function. This function gets the red, green and blue values of each pixel of the image by looping through its width and height, incrementing the RGB value each time. When finished, we average each out by dividing each colour value by the amount of pixels in the image count. We then work out the brightness of each image by calculating the square root of each colour value when added together.

```
    // Add these values to the appropriate colour array.
    var obj:Object      = new Object();
    obj.bmpData         = bmpData;
    obj.bright          = bright;

    if(red > green && red > blue){
        if(bright >= 0 && bright <= 129){
            __arrRedDark.push(obj);
        }
        else if(bright >= 130 && bright <= 259){
            __arrRedMid.push(obj);
        }
        else if(bright >= 260 && bright <= 450){
            __arrRedLight.push(obj);
        }
    }
    else if(green > red && green > blue){
        if(bright >= 0 && bright <= 129){
            __arrGreenDark.push(obj);
        }
        else if(bright >= 130 && bright <= 259){
            __arrGreenMid.push(obj);
        }
        else if(bright >= 260 && bright <= 450){
            __arrGreenLight.push(obj);
        }
    }
    else if(blue > red && blue > green){
        if(bright >= 0 && bright <= 129){
```

08_____ Now we work out if the image is predominantly red, green, blue or grey with some simple if tests. We then find out how bright it is with more simple if tests. The brightness is in three brackets: light, mid or dark. The lower the number, the darker something is. With these values, we store the image bitmap data in the correct array to use when we call the createMosaic function later in the tutorial. Once all the images are loaded and stored in their arrays, we sort each array so they start from the darkest image to the lightest.

→

```
private function startCamera():void
{
    // Activate the webcam.
    __camera = Camera.getCamera();

    // Add a listener to the camera that looks out for activity.
    // If there is activity then we call the activityHandler function.
    __camera.addEventListener(ActivityEvent.ACTIVITY, activityHandler);
    __camera.setMode(__cameraWidth, __cameraHeight, 20, false);
    __camera.setQuality(1, 0);

    // Create a new video object and add it to the videoMC movie clip.
    __video = new Video(__cameraWidth, __cameraHeight);
    __video.attachCamera(__camera);

    // Brighten the webcam image. Play around with these values or remove completely.
    TweenMax.to(__video, 0, {colorMatrixFilter:{contrast:1.5, brightness:1.5}});
}
```

09_____We now start the webcam. We set up the camera, and set up a listener to listen out for any camera activity. Create a video object, attach the camera to the video object and, using TweenMax, brighten up the video. When the listener detects camera activity, set __camPlaying to true and start the pixelating process.

```
private function activityHandler(e:ActivityEvent):void {
    // The camera has started so we can remove the listener that looks out for activity.
    __camera.removeEventListener(ActivityEvent.ACTIVITY, activityHandler);

    if(e.activating){
        if(!__camPlaying){
            __camPlaying = true;

            var pauseID:uint = setTimeout(startPixelate, 1000);
        }
    }
}

private function startPixelate():void {
    addEventListener(Event.ENTER_FRAME, pixelate);
}

private function pixelate(evt:Event):void {
    // Create a bitmap copy of the webcam image.
    __videoBitmapData.draw(__video);

    // Create the mosaic.
    createMosaic();
}
```

10_____The startPixelate function sets up an ENTER_FRAME event listener. It calls the pixelate function based on the available frame rate. In the pixelate function, take a bitmap copy of the webcam image using the __videoBitmapData.draw(__video); line of code. Call the createMosaic function.

```
private function createMosaic():void {
    // Remove the last mosaic holding movieclip.
    if(__mosaicMC != null){
        removeChild(__mosaicMC);
        __mosaicMC = null;
    }

    // Create a new mosaic holding movieclip.
    __mosaicMC = new MovieClip();
```

11_____The createMosaic function is where we bring everything together. Firstly, create an empty Movie Clip to hold all the mosaic pieces. This is called __mosaicMC. As this function is being called repeatedly, we need to check if a __mosaicMC exists already. If one does, then we need to delete it as we don't want our SWF being clogged up by hundreds of complex mosaics.

```
private function createMosaic():void {
    // Remove the last mosaic holding movieclip.
    if(__mosaicMC != null){
        removeChild(__mosaicMC);
        __mosaicMC = null;
    }

    // Create a new mosaic holding movieclip.
    __mosaicMC = new MovieClip();

    // These for loops are based on the camera width and height values.
    // It loops through each pixel of the webcam over a specified range (__pixelSize) and works out it's pixel
    // It then works out the average colour of the pixel and its brightness.
    for (var xNum:uint = 0; xNum < __cameraWidth; xNum += __pixelSize)
    {
        for (var yNum:uint = 0; yNum < __cameraHeight; yNum += __pixelSize)
        {
            var pixelColour:Number = __videoBitmapData.getPixel(xNum, yNum);
            var red:Number    = getRed(pixelColour);
            var green:Number  = getGreen(pixelColour);
            var blue:Number   = getBlue(pixelColour);
            var bright:Number = getBright(red, green, blue);

            var bmp:Bitmap;

            var col:String;

            // Based on the average pixel colour and brightness we now take a random image from the appropriate
            if(red > green && red > blue){
                if(bright >= 0 && bright <= 129){
                    if(__arrRedDark.length > 0){
```

12_____We then get the pixel colour from the webcam based on the __pixelSize size. As the __pixelSize in this tutorial is set at 16, we get each 16th pixel colour value. The __pixelSize value can be played around with. The smaller the number, the more detail you'll get in the mosaic. However, the smaller the number is, the slower it can become as it has more pixels it needs to evaluate.

```
for (var yNum:uint = 0; yNum < __cameraHeight; yNum += __pixelSize)
{
    var pixelColour:Number  = __videoBitmapData.getPixel(xNum, yNum);
    var red:Number     = getRed(pixelColour);
    var green:Number   = getGreen(pixelColour);
    var blue:Number    = getBlue(pixelColour);
    var bright:Number  = getBright(red, green, blue);

    var bmp:Bitmap;
```

```
private function getRed(pixelColour:Number):Number {
    return pixelColour >> 16 & 0xFF;
}

private function getGreen(pixelColour:Number):Number {
    return pixelColour >> 8 & 0xFF;
}

private function getBlue(pixelColour:Number):Number {
    return pixelColour & 0xFF;
}

private function getBright(red:Number, green:Number, blue:Number):Number {
    return Math.round(Math.sqrt(red*red + green*green + blue*blue));
}
}
```

13_____Then we get the red, green and blue values from the pixel colour of the webcam. Do this by calling the getRed, getGreen and getBlue functions, and passing them the pixelColour variable value. We also get the brightness of the pixel by calling the getBright function and passing it the red, green and blue variable values.

```
var bmp:Bitmap;

var col:String;

// Based on the average pixel colour and brightness we now take a random image from the appropriate array.
if(red > green && red > blue){
    if(bright >= 0 && bright <= 129){
        if(__arrRedDark.length > 0){
            bmp = new Bitmap(__arrRedDark[Math.ceil(Math.random()*__arrRedDark.length) - 1].bmpData);
        }
    }
    else if(bright >= 130 && bright <= 259){
        if(__arrRedMid.length > 0){
            bmp = new Bitmap(__arrRedMid[Math.ceil(Math.random()*__arrRedMid.length) - 1].bmpData);
        }
    }
    else if(bright >= 260 && bright <= 450){
        if(__arrRedLight.length > 0){
            bmp = new Bitmap(__arrRedLight[Math.ceil(Math.random()*__arrRedLight.length) - 1].bmpData);
        }
    }
}
else if(green > red && green > blue){
    if(bright >= 0 && bright <= 129){
        if(__arrGreenDark.length > 0){
            bmp = new Bitmap(__arrGreenDark[Math.ceil(Math.random()*__arrGreenDark.length) - 1].bmpData);
        }
    }
    else if(bright >= 130 && bright <= 259){
        if(__arrGreenMid.length > 0){
            bmp = new Bitmap(__arrGreenMid[Math.ceil(Math.random()*__arrGreenMid.length) - 1].bmpData);
        }
    }
    else if(bright >= 260 && bright <= 450){
        if(__arrGreenLight.length > 0){
            bmp = new Bitmap(__arrGreenLight[Math.ceil(Math.random()*__arrGreenLight.length) - 1].bmpData);
```

14_____With these RGB and bright values, we can work out which array we need to draw the image from. This is done with if tests in the same way as in Step 8. For instance, if the webcam pixel we are evaluating is red, we then test if its brightness is dark, mid or light. If it's dark, we grab a random bitmap from the __arrRedDark array.

```
            if(bmp != null){
                // Change the size of the random bitmap image.
                bmp.width  = __pixelSize;
                bmp.height = __pixelSize;

                // Position the random bitmap image.
                bmp.x = xNum;
                bmp.y = yNum;

                // Add the the random bitmap image to the mosaic holding movieclip.
                __mosaicMC.addChild(bmp);
            }
        }
    }

    // Flip the resulting mosaic image so it appears the right way round.
    __mosaicMC.scaleX = -1;
    __mosaicMC.x      = __cameraWidth;

    // Add the mosaic image to the stage.
    addChild(__mosaicMC);
}
```

15_____Now you have your bitmap, add it to the __mosaicMC Movie Clip. Before doing this, the width and height of the bitmap is set to the __pixelSize variable value (in this case, 16px). Then position it based on the xNum and yNum. Once the for loop is complete and the small pieces are added to the __mosaicMC Movie Clip, the __mosaic MC is flipped by setting its x scale to -1 the repositioned, so what you see is the correct way around. As this is set up with an ENTER_FRAME listener, this process is repeated.

Save up to 40%
in our fantastic January Sale!

Inspiration Workshop

Spiral Studio's photo compositions

Darren Hopes builds moody, striking images with his own photographs, a hint of nostalgia and a touch of darkness

__The designer

Darren Hopes

Producing commercial work under his given name, Darren Hopes also creates personal, artistic pieces under the pseudonym Spiral Studio. His interest in visual storytelling was sparked at an early age by publications such as *2000 AD*. He went on to study design photography at Exeter University, gaining a first-class honours. Now an illustrator, Hopes is represented by Central Illustration Agency.
www.athomeinspace.com

__The project

Fantastical photo constructions

Working in his Spiral Studio style, Darren Hopes produces work that verges on the dark and surreal. He likes to build an image gradually rather than stop at a plain photograph, and this approach results in painterly, illustrative works. For Hopes, working with photographs as a base media is as versatile as drawing or painting itself. Recent work has delved into model-making, which brings a new element to the creative mix.

Media
—Power Mac G5
—Nikon D2X
—Nikon SB-800 flash
—Various lenses
—Photoshop CS4
—Milliput
—Various off-camera lights and reflectors
—Air-drying clay
—Paint
—Pencils

The Spiral Studio style was originally the result of a duality that existed in my portfolio. I've always worked with an amalgamation of painting and photography, but as my illustrative style developed it became flatter, more graphic and certainly more painterly. This left me feeling like I was missing an overtly photographic aesthetic. I had, after all, trained in photography.

With my more graphic illustrative stuff proving to be a commercial success, I wanted a break from that world, and so started working on pieces that were more about my photography. A very personal language emerged, and I decided to separate it from my folio and give it a life of its own under the moniker Spiral Studio.

Muse laid bare

The works in my *Muse* series mostly began life in my sketchbooks and writings. I jot down thoughts and ideas, often from very disparate sources, and, much like writing a story, an idea for an image gradually begins to formulate. The *Muse* series began with my desire to try my hand at artistic nude imagery, but I have been steering it away from its overtly erotic beginnings. The whole erotic side to the work grew more than I intended after I was nominated

01

03-04 In personal
series *Graphique*,
Hopes explores
found objects and
the photographed
female form as
montage on a
flat background

Spiral's studio

My studio is in rural Cornwall, and I think that influences my work. From my window I can view little snatches of nature that I would never witness if I worked in the city centre. Foxes, snakes, bats (in the studio once), lizards, newts, swans – an endless parade of nature passes by.

Aside from books, prints and generally interesting visual reference, my studio is populated by the old toys and figures that I collect for use in my work, and bits of twigs and dead insects that I have found. My wife refuses to open any draws for fear of what she might find! I am a collector of debris and outdated junk. It inspires me, and those things are the words of my visual language. 90 per cent of the time, there is music playing in the studio too. I'm very heavily influenced by music.

02

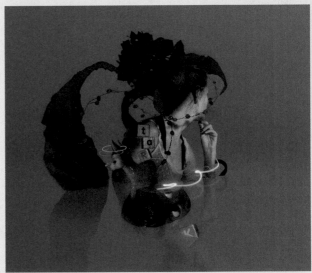

04

01 'The Dressmaker' is one section of a triptych created for the *Muse* series. It has also been sold as a print by Central Illustration Agency

02 Recent image **'Circus Show'** was created as part of a Central Illustration Agency exhibition. In it, Hopes introduced model-making to his image creation process

03

and then shortlisted as a finalist for Erotic Photographer of the Year in 2007. Inevitably I continued to create more erotic images. Lately I am making that side of it more incidental, although by its nature the *Muse* series will retain a subtle, sexy feel. For example, the latest image, 'Circus Show', has no nudity but I do think the pose is feminine, and so continues the theme.

Much of the *Muse* series is about memories and time passing; life is a little dreamlike, especially memories. I do play up this surreal side with the ghost-like quality of some elements. Things appear to be not quite there, and I use perspective distortions as well. I think our memories of the past are distorted and perhaps not quite as true as we might think. Aside from that, I just have a lot of fun with costumes!

Form functions

The images in my *Spiral Graphique* collection are a little less philosophical and more about form. It's an experimental area really, but is leading to commissions. I have always been inspired by nature and forms in nature, so the inclusion of flowers and leaves is purely the result of what I am drawn to.

'Graphique 01' (image 3, pictured left) was the first image, and was entirely experimental. I liked the shapes that the cluster of objects was making, and wanted to push that further by presenting these clusters on a blank backdrop to emphasise the shape of the group. To be honest, the objects you see in the →

05 The piece **'Superfreakynight-out'** is part of Spiral Studio's *Muse* series, which puts an erotic slant on the surreal worlds within our dreams and memories

06 'Put Me on a Planet', created for Steel Tiger Records, is an example of Spiral Studio work done to commission. Hopes was given free reign on the image

07 "I like to get right back to my photographic roots and create, albeit with a bit of manipulation, a still life," says Hopes. This piece is number one of his **still life series**

06

05

→ image were knocking about in my studio and I just photographed them and explored what I had in mind. There was no grand plan apart from, 'I wonder how that would look?'

The storyteller
Of course, it's ingrained in me to want to inject narrative into my work. I think that was developed further in images like 'Graphique 5' and the Jstars CD cover. The little characters that I find in junk shops really aid that; they have a life of their own, perhaps in part due to their age. Each of them had a whole life story before I picked them up, and it shows. It adds something timeless to the images.

When beginning an image, I often have a good idea of the figures and toys I'm going to use as I have them around the studio. If I need a specific character, animal or figure, I will put the image on the back burner until I find the right thing. For client work, I may hire a model if there is budget. My wife and friends or family have also modelled for various pieces. The image may also require some landscape photography. I jot down locations or, sometimes, I'll sketch something and keep my eyes open for a suitable location. I'm looking for a deserted petrol station at the moment.

Rough it up
I'll do sketches to get an idea of composition and relationship between the landscape and the central figure. I might have an idea of the pose but I do try to remain open to what might happen in the photographic process. That way, if something cool happens spontaneously while I'm shooting, I won't be railroaded in my vision.

Usually I take quite a lot of shots and edit the images down to the best ones. I then work on the central character, touch it

07

up and add things like tattoos. Next I work on the backdrop and build the image, adding elements, layers of colour and lighting. It's quite intuitive at this stage, with no real rules, just an idea of how I want the image to feel and what I want to put across in the narrative.

I am pretty much entirely Photoshop-based as far as software is concerned. I always use casts of light. A blank light that I overlay in Photoshop can create a cast that holds the image together and distracts from the fact that the light in the landscape may differ from the light in the studio where the model and other elements were shot.

Ironically, Spiral Studio has proven very popular in the commercial world. Happily, it does not seem to be getting watered down – clients are, on the whole, quite happy for me to keep it dark and surreal. Having said that, a few book covers I did recently called for a brighter approach, but I was really quite happy with the results, which surprised me.

Influences
The Starn Twins, Joel-Peter Witkin and Tracy Holland: These early influences opened my eyes to what could be done with photography in a constructed sense.

Dave McKean: Anyone studying in the area of illustrative or constructed photography in the '90s would have been aware of him. He went into Photoshop at a time when my work was mostly handmade, so that was important.

William Latham: He sparked my long-term interest in organic and natural forms.

Bettina Rheims and Aaron Hawks: These creatives influenced me when I experimented with erotica.

Frida Kahlo: Her work was an influence on both my photography and my illustration.

James Jean: This contemporary illustrator is just incredible.

The in-depth guide for creative professionals

computer

arts

projects Issue 132

January 2010
computerarts.co.uk

A DECADE OF DESIGN

2000–2009 How 10 years changed the face of design, and what we can expect next

PLUS: Stay ahead of the game with our expert forecast for design trends in 2010

<u>InDesign CS3 or later</u>

Creating tables in InDesign

Whether importing data or typing it onto your document, the process needn't be complex. **Jo Gulliver** brings simplicity to the table

A table is a great way of presenting sequential or categorised information within a layout. There's no need for tables to be difficult to construct, though, as InDesign enables you to create and edit them simply. It's even possible to import tables from Microsoft Excel and edit these in the same, easy way.

You can either create a table from scratch or by importing existing text. In this tutorial I'll show you both of these techniques. It's good to remember that a table in InDesign exists within a text frame, so is editable with the Text tool. You can also use the usual type adjustments in your table, such as aligning text to the baseline grid, offsetting type, changing the colour and font – the list goes on. It's best just to experiment with all your options!

Jo Gulliver
__ As *Computer Arts'* PPA Designer of the Year-nominated art editor, Jo's month typically entails commissioning cover artists and photo shoots from all over the world, and laying out features and tutorials. www. computerarts.co.uk

Time needed
10 minutes

Skills
__Understanding Text Wrap options
__Editing wraparound paths

01____ To create a table from scratch, draw a text frame, select the frame with the Text tool then go to Table>Insert Table. The Insert Table box pops up, from which you can choose your number of rows and columns. The Header and Footer Rows options are useful when you have a table that's split across columns or pages, as crucial table heading information is repeated.

02____ Using the Text tool, enter your copy. At this stage you may want to edit the table, so select Window>Type & Tables>Table to access your Tables palette. This will give you all the tools you need to make changes to your table, including enabling you to insert and delete rows.

03____ To turn existing text into a table, highlight the text and select Table>Convert Text to Table. The Convert Text to Table dialog box will open, and you can select the characters you'll use to break copy into rows and columns. The Number of Columns option will only display when it's not possible to determine the number of columns by the defined character (for instance, if your copy uses tabs to mark both the row and column breaks, you will need to enter the number of columns needed manually). If importing text to the table, take time to check that the information has the correct characters included to mark the column and row breaks. For example, use paragraph breaks for column breaks and tabs for rows.

04____ Change the heading in the table to a continuous line by merging cells; this option is in the drop-down menu on your Tables panel. You can easily change the size of rows and columns by placing the Text tool over the gridline you want to move; this will bring up a double-ended arrow which indicates that it's safe to move the grid lines.

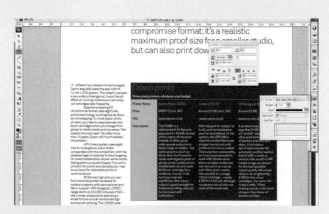

05____ Continue making changes to your table by editing the colours and fonts until you have the correct style. You can hide or show particular gridlines by clicking on the blue lines in the row and columns preview box found on the right-hand side of the Tool options bar. You'll find a larger view of this in your Stroke panel.

Design fundamentals
Essential software skills for creative professionals

Illustrator and Flash CS3 or later

Smoothing the Flash/ Illustrator relationship

Work seamlessly between Illustrator and Flash to save yourself precious studio time. **Paul Wyatt** shows you how

Flash and Illustrator love each other. They may have had the occasional rift over the years, what with compatibility being an issue at times, but they now work smoothly side by side, enabling you to create stunning vector artwork and animate it in Flash without any headaches. The best way to work with Illustrator and Flash is to keep both programs open and flip between them. This way you can easily update Illustrator artwork before simply pasting it back into Flash. In this tutorial, I'll show you how to do just that in a handful of steps.

Paul Wyatt
__ Paul Wyatt has created websites, animation work and broadcast creative for clients such as Talkback Thames, D&AD, Virgin Media and the BBC. To find out more, visit www. paulwyatt.co.uk

On the disc
The files relating to this tutorial can be located in DiscContents\ Resources\AiFlash

Time needed
10 minutes

Skills
——Symbol creation
——Using dynamic and input text
——Importing Illustrator artboards

01_____ Planning your Illustrator artwork will save you precious time in Flash later. You can now define artwork as a specific symbol type – Graphic or Movie Clip. Flash remembers the Flash symbol name and type. From the disc, open symbols.ai and select Window>Symbols. Hit 'V', then select and drag the building into the Symbols panel. In the Symbol Options pop-up box, name the symbol 'Building'. Set it as a Movie Clip.

02_____ Copying and pasting artwork into Flash is easy. Select the Buildings and Sky symbols, select Edit>Copy and flip to Flash. Create a new document and select Edit>Paste. In the Paste pop-up, check 'Paste using AI File Importer preferences' and 'Maintain layers'. Preserving layers is essential here, as motion tweens won't work with multiple elements on a layer. Click OK to paste the artwork into the FLA file.

My title

03_____ In Illustrator you can define Flash text as 'dynamic', 'static' or 'input'. Select the type layer 'My title' in text.ai on the disc, and choose Window>Type>Flash type. If your type is set as Dynamic Text, give it an instance name so it can be controlled with ActionScript. Dynamic Text enables you to pull text from an XML feed into a text field in Flash using the specified font – useful when content needs to be updated frequently. You can copy and paste your text element from Illustrator to Flash.

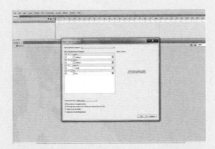

04_____ As well as being able to paste individual elements from Illustrator to Flash, you can import scenes containing multiple layers and elements. Open Flash and create a new document. Flash will set the document size to match the Illustrator file for you. Select File> Import>Import to Stage, then select scene.ai. This will open the AI Importer dialog box, where you can set options for your imported artwork. The maximum size of the Flash stage is 2880x2880px. Rescale your artwork in Illustrator if you need to, and re-import.

05_____ The key to importing Illustrator artboards into Flash is to make sure that any extraneous layers are removed from the original Illustrator file. To avoid bloated Flash files, clean up your Illustrator file before importing. Check the 'Set stage to same size as Illustrator artboard' box. Select 'sky', 'building1' and 'building2' and choose 'Create Movie Clip' from the Import options. Check 'Convert to Flash layers' and hit OK to import the file. Your stage is resized to match the Illustrator file, and all your layers are replicated and ready for animating.

Cinema 4D v9 or later

Explosive motion graphics: Part one

Have a blast creating an animated graphic sequence in Cinema 4D and After Effects. In the first of two tutorials, **Alex Donne Johnson** explains how

Over this tutorial and next month's sequel, I will be looking at how to create an entire motion graphics piece that could well be used as an ident. This month I will focus on creating an explosive scene with a neon, electro feel in Cinema 4D. I'll be using photographs of people jumping, compositing them in 3D space in a way that makes them look like they have been caught in suspended animation at the point of an explosion. Next month we will look at how to make After Effects work with Cinema 4D's Camera Data using the RPF export function. A familiarity with Cinema 4D's basic functions – such as the Move, Rotate and Scale tools, and the different editing modes such as Model, Point and Edge – will be useful for this tutorial.

Alex Donne Johnson
__ Spending his days working freelance for clients such as Adidas, Levi's and Rolls Royce, by night Johnson works as a VJ and has performed at clubs and festivals across Europe. See more of his work at www. vectormeldrew.com

On the disc
The file accompanying this tutorial can be located in DiscContents\ Resources\Motion

Time needed
6 hours

Skills
__ Creating a
  3D scene
__ Animating a
  camera in
  3D space
__ Creating basic
  materials
__ Creating
  3D objects
__ Rendering

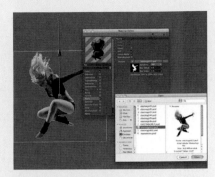

01_____Firstly, the time consuming part. Find a selection of images and cut them out so they are .psd files with transparent backgrounds. The images I've used here are from a collection on iStockPhoto called 'Jumping People'. Try to make sure the width and height of the canvas are equal.

02_____In Cinema 4D, go to Objects>Primitive>Plane and, in Object Properties, make the width and height segments both '1'. Create a new material with Color and Alpha properties, and set the Texture setting of both to one of the PSDs created in Step 1. Apply this material by dragging it onto the plane.

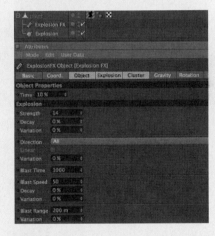

03_____Press C to 'make editable' then, making sure you are in Edge mode, go to Structure>Knife and cut your image up in the way you want it to be blown apart. Then go to Objects>Deformation>Explosion and make the Strength 1% (or more).

04_____Next add the Explosion FX and amend the values to Object: Time = 10%; Explosion: Strength = 14m; Cluster: Thickness = 10m. Do a test render. It's good to play around with these settings for each image and experiment a bit.

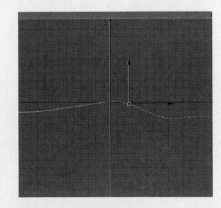

05_____Now repeat Steps 2 to 4 for each of the other images (to save time, you can just copy and paste the explosion effects). Now create a new scene to make things easier for the next step.

06_____Draw a spline using Object>Create Spline>B Spline then click from left to right in the 'Top' view on the grid. Make it slightly curvy as you do it by clicking in different positions. We will now use this as the path for the camera. →

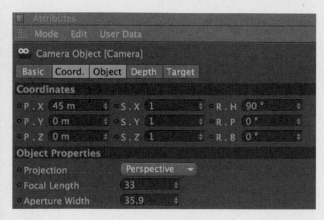

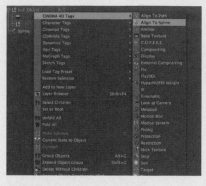

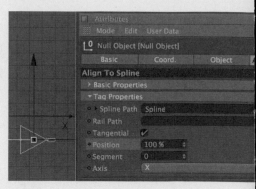

07_____Go to Objects>Scene>Target Camera and change the coordinates of the camera to: X = 45, Y = 0 and Z = 0. Make sure that in Object Properties the Projection is set to 'Perspective'. Select the camera and target in the objects window, Right/Ctrl+click and go to Group Objects.

08_____Right/Ctrl+click on the Null Object you just created. Go to Cinema 4D Tags>Align To Spline, then click and drag the spline into the Spline Path field. Check the Tangential box. You may have to change the axis to X depending on where your camera is pointing.

09_____In the same window we will now animate the Position field. Increase the size of the timeline to 350 frames, and at Frame 350 add a keyframe to make the position 1%. At Frame 0 make it 100%. The camera should now animate along the line.

10_____Now copy and paste the exploded planes from the previous steps into this new scene. To save render times and make the scene less cluttered, select them all, Right/Ctrl+click, go to 'Current State to Object' then delete the old ones.

11_____Now individually rotate and position each of the different images along the path. You can scrub the timeline to check if it looks good in a particular position or not. Try to get the images all the way down until the end.

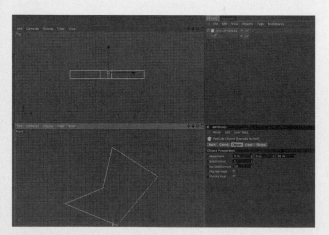

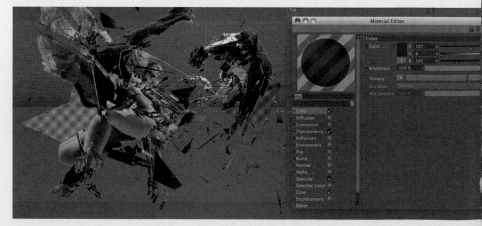

12_____Create some extra debris by going to Object>Create Spline>Linear and make some random shapes. Then extrude by going to Object>NURBS>Extrude NURBS. Place them in the scene where you think they work best.

13_____Create a new texture with these properties ticked: Color, Transparency, Specular, Glow. Choose the same colour for the Color and Transparency options. Repeat this step to create a few different coloured materials then add them to the NURBs you just created.

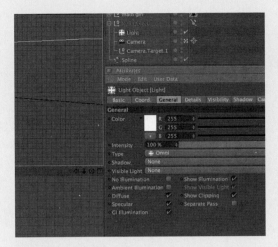

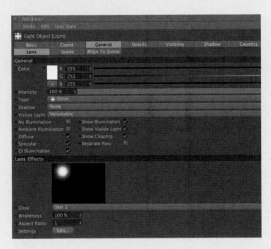

14____Create some lighting by going to Object>Scene>Lighting. Do this twice, placing one light in the same group as the camera and positioning it directly in front of the camera.

15____For the other light, change the attributes to General: Visible Light = Volumetric. Then go to the Lens tab and have a look through the options for Glow and Reflex. Place this light somewhere near the centre of your composition, halfway down the original spline.

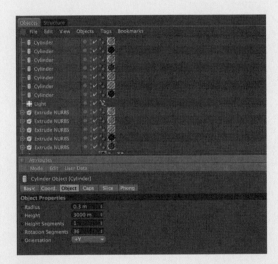

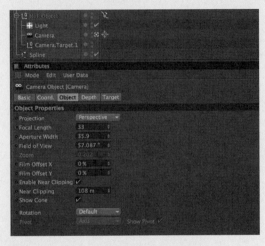

16____To create the laser lines, I have gone to Object>Primitive>Cylinder and given it a radius of 0.3m and a height of 3000m. I have then added one of the materials from Step 13 and placed a few randomly around the scene.

17____To make the start of the camera movement more dynamic, animate the Focal Length with keyframes of a value of 2 on Frame 0 and 33 on Frame 90.

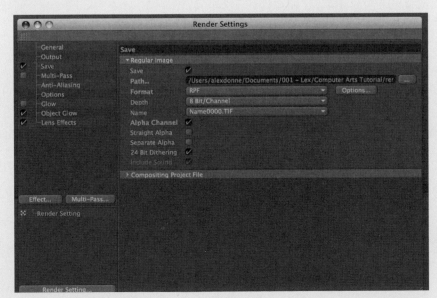

18____Now go to Render>Render Settings and use these settings: Output =1024x576; Frame Range = 0-250; Save Format = RPF (Alpha Channel checked); Anti-aliasing = Best; Effects = Object Glow and Lens Effects. Click Render>Render to Picture Viewer.

Alex Donne Johnson
Favourite past projects

Adidas Slam Van – August 2007
This was my first Adidas project. It's a Chevrolet van with a hoop on the back, promoting basketball to London's youth.

Bristol Festival logo – November 2007
I created the logo design and branding for Bristol's summer festival.

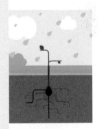

Apple Pips music video – March 2009
Motion graphics/ animation piece for forward-thinking record label Apple Pips, following the life cycle of an apple seed.

2562 *Unbalance* album artwork – August 2009
Album cover art for a Dutch dubstep producer, made using Cinema 4D and Photoshop.

Adidas 'About to Blow' poster – September 2009
One of nine poster designs for Adidas and the Olympic 2012 committee, plus a motion graphics piece that this tutorial was inspired by.

Brief Encounter

The creation of *The Google Story*

Director **Nick Scott** of Nick Scott Studio leafs through the making of the new brand film charting the life of one of the world's most prominent companies

__ The designer
Nick Scott
Nick Scott is a London-based creative director and film director at Nick Scott Studio Ltd. Scott joined branding firm Static 2358 in 1998 and went on to produce branding and idents for some of the world's largest brands, gaining wide acclaim and international awards. Subsequently, he co-founded Sydney creative agency Maud, which worked on diverse projects for clients and agencies including Daihatsu, M&C Saatchi and Saatchi & Saatchi. Returning to London in 2006, Scott formed the widely awarded Nick Scott Studio as a vehicle for concept and production work across film, branding and animation.
www.krop.com/nickscottstudio

__ The brief
The Google Story brand film
The project began when I got a call from Rachna Suri, the executive producer for Across The Pond/ Google Creative Hub. I'd been referred by Chris Boyle – a friend of mine who was directing a zombie movie at the time! – as Google was looking for someone to conceive and produce a brand film to encapsulate its epic rise. I was immensely interested in documenting such a modern icon's progress; it felt like quite a responsibility to get it right. The end goal was a multi-use brand film.

Media
—— Canon 5D Mk II
—— Photoshop
—— Illustrator
—— After Effects
—— Cinema 4D
—— Pen
—— Paper
—— Tape
—— Stickers

 **Obviously Google is pretty immense in terms of its exponential growth scale, so our initial conversations revolved around how we could create something that enabled the viewer to digest so much information yet feel compelled to stick with the piece.** Furthermore, the budget was very challenging (granted, the words 'challenging budget' and 'Google' don't sit too well together...)

I really like telling great stories, irrespective of medium and style, be it via a cinematic shot-based piece or a lo-fi animation. As Google tends to like a quirky, lo-fi aesthetic, it soon became apparent that some kind of animation or shot/animation hybrid was the way to go, so we came up with the idea of producing a scrapbook. Obviously there are a lot of scrapbook-style executions

01

Nick Scott's Studio

The studio is small – a move is on the cards in early 2010. However, there's an honesty and quaintness to it in that the world seems to be righting itself along a 'small is beautiful' structure anyhow. We also share and have a strong partnership with CGI/VFX studio Darkside, and we're mutually interested in exploring a creative, production and CGI model. In these changing times, we've had some real successes by pooling strong creative thinking and execution along with cutting-edge post and VFX.

We have a few Apple desktop machines running the usual software, as well as a small green screen set-up for tests and such. In addition, we also work with other talented directors, animators or compositors, depending on what we have on the go.

01-02 Nick Scott and collaborator Chris Angelkov put a fresh spin on the trusted **scrapbook presentation concept** through their innovative and lively treatment of Google's past records and statistics

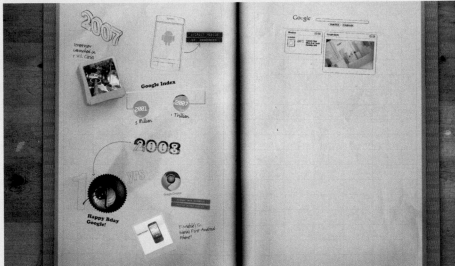

02

out there so we were aware that our concept was not wholly innovative. However, we thought that in the execution we could try a few things out that may be more unique.

The search begins

In terms of developing the idea, the guys at Google were immensely trusting and gave us a massive amount of freedom with regards to sketching out the concept. It was obvious that the piece was going to be pretty long in animation terms (the final piece comes in at over two minutes) so we didn't really have the luxury of the shot-for-shot breakdown that may be expected when working traditionally with an agency or on a TV spot, for instance.

Firstly, I wrote a treatment and produced some style frames of what we were thinking so that the various departments of Google could get a broad outline of what was being undertaken. After a couple of conversations voicing concerns that the piece should not be 'too slick', it was full steam ahead for production.

I drafted in my good friend (and frequent collaborator) Chris Angelkov to help flesh out the idea. Chris and I had had early successful collaborations such as working on the SI Futures music video that toured globally with work from the likes of Michel Gondry and Spike Jonze. We had roughly two weeks to make two minutes of HD content, and I knew Chris would be a great sounding board and partner in producing an ambitious amount by such a tight deadline.

Mapping Google

So began a journey involving copious amounts of caffeine, sketches and dialogue trying to break down Google's mammoth volume of achievement and stats into a quirky and compelling narrative. →

03-04 A short deadline meant that the team had to **trial production techniques** as they went along. One successful trick was using pieces of gaffer tape to hold the scrapbook's various components in place

05 Stop-frame elements are peppered through the film, showing balls of paper unravelling, and cash and floppy discs piling up

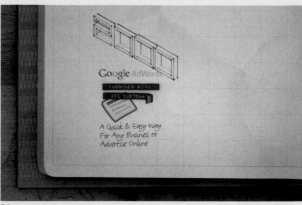

04

Influences
David Fincher, Jean-Pierre Jeunet, Sergio Leone, Chuck Palahniuk, John Barry, Martin Parr and Kraftwerk.

03

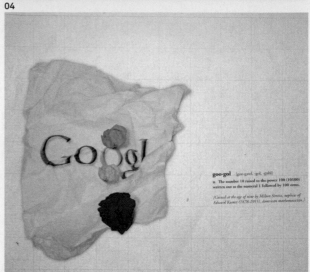

05

→ We interpreted our coffee-time sketches into a diagrammatic storyboard of how we proposed to illustrate the points of the narrative. Liaising with Rachna and the Google guys via email and over the phone, we first thought of making the whole thing shot-based and using wires to turn the pages before incorporating the CG elements later. Initially we thought this lo-fi look would be really clean and filmic. However, we actually found that it looked sort of bland and didn't add any more value than a GCI book – which of course would be easier to manipulate and integrate with CG elements. So, in the end, we built a 3D book and decided to shoot the desk and the elements before marrying it all together in composite.

Once this route was decided, fixing on how we wanted to make the component parts became quite an organic process. For instance, we shot stop-frame elements for the balls of paper unravelling, we used bits of gaffer tape to hold the items of the scrapbook in place, we filmed ink blots to incorporate into the spray can section, and we generated much of the inked typographic headings using a Toon Shader in Cinema 4D. It really was a hugely mixed-media piece.

Results listing
What became quite challenging was that we were working at up to 8000 pixels wide – we needed to oversize many of the assets so that we could cut in close and have the resolution still stand up at HD, so the processing and rendering times became pretty hefty.

Google was hugely trusting, as we were so flat out trying to produce the assets that 'work in progress' tests were either

Visual CV
In pictures: a guide to the career and work of our Technique writers

Nick Scott
The director and studio founder selects five of his favourite past projects

Playjam commercials – 2001
The objective was to make everyday, mundane challenges seem epic. I love the cinematic tone and the fact that the ads received mixed responses from different viewers. In contrast to some of my more FX-heavy work, they are in some ways actually more 'me' in terms of just trying to tell the story in the most beautifully simple way possible.

NRMA ad spot – 2005
This was made at my old agency in Sydney, and was commissioned by M&C Saatchi. We had multi-locations and a typographic message to convey across the whole spot. I was really happy with the dramatic and cinematic quality of it. It's possibly one of my favourite pieces, just because of its subtlety and the deftness involved.

06-07 The whole film is **shot from above**, with certain shots closing in. To maintain HD quality, Scott and Angelkov worked at up to **8000px wide**

08 There is scope for development on a potential follow-up film charting Google's next decade. Scott suggests that a **broadening of the**

book's setting and the angles used for shooting the film could be brought into play on a sequel

06

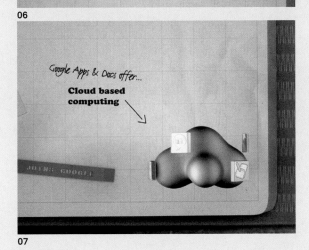

07

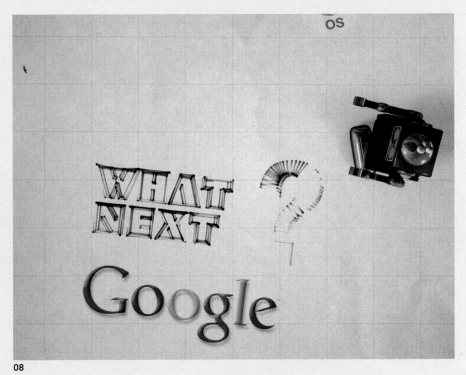

08

nonexistent or arrived with Google very late in the day. We would send 20- to 30-second chunks through as and when they were completed, and then make a priority list of changes – we were acutely aware that we needed to press on, and that some minor gripes would have to be addressed later than the bigger brand no-nos, particularly if we were going to meet the deadline. At times it was relatively stressful, as we were always up against it, generating content at this size and duration under such a crazy deadline. Ideally, we would usually pre-vis or board the whole thing, but again the time and budget didn't really cater for that.

Amidst all this, however, the guys at Google were really cool and had nerves of steel, trusting our judgement in terms of content generation. So after quite a few late nights, weekends and TV (or computer) dinners, we delivered the brand film ready for an

important conference. Given more time and a greater budget, I'd have liked to have shot more, perhaps given the book a wider place in which to exist. I'd also probably have gone down the route of shooting the book from more than just a top-down view, and perhaps had the iconography of the book interacting with the world at large – perhaps text from the book being written on walls or posters. That said, I think the constraints give the film a focused charm, and comments we've received about it have been pretty favourable, as well as it getting over 300,000 YouTube hits in a matter of days (see the film at www.youtube.com/watch?v=EjN5avRvApk)! I'm pretty pleased with it, and it fulfils my goal to keep telling compelling brand stories, whether that's shooting with a 50-man crew, a lo-fi animation/stop-frame hybrid or whatever the medium may be.

Pimms 'Summer Pursuits' spots – 2007
I created these spots for Agency Republic. They were hectic but great fun to make – I was really pleased with the tone that they struck. The work went on to be commended at the Campaign awards.

Network Rail promo film – 2008
The agency, Pretzel, needed a film to promote the launch of Network Rail's new £34bn rail line. We conceived a spot around a blueprint coming to life on a drawing board. We worked with trusted partners Darkside, and the piece went on to greatly exceed client expectations.

Land Rover LRX launch film – 2008
Nick Scott Studio was asked by Imagination to make the global launch film for Land Rover's flagship LRX. The piece premiered to wide acclaim at The Detroit Motor Show and went on to win a BIMA 2008 in the Best Film & Animation category.

BoopFest

London
23-26 November 09

Music
Film
Design
Comedy

Tickets £125

Photoshop and Illustrator
CS3 or later

Be clear through abstraction

Gordon Reid shows how embarking on an abstract design doesn't mean you have to leave clear communication at the door

In an evolving world where the boundaries between design and illustration seem to draw ever closer, it is important to remember some of the fundamentals. Particularly in terms of design, getting your message across clearly is vital.

More and more festivals are cropping up, regardless of time of year, location or budget, and the posters for these can provide a great canvas for a designer to get really creative. But the fact that there are so many festival posters means that the image needs to stand out and the message needs to be communicated clearly. In this tutorial, I will run you through the creation of an eye-catching collage using retro found imagery and stock images, blended with a number of handy techniques that will guide you in creating an abstract piece of design that communicates well.

Gordon Reid
__ Middle Boop is the moniker of designer, illustrator and blogger Reid. As well as working for clients including record labels 4AD and Bella Union, and bands such as Deerhunter, Prefuse 73 and Of Montreal, Reid has had animations shown at the BFI and runs the *Middle Boop* fanzine. See more of his work at www. middleboop.com

On the disc
The files accompanying this tutorial can be located in DiscContents\ Resources\ Abstraction

Time needed
2-3 hours

Skills
__ Creating retro-look images
__ Blending vectors with found imagery
__ Merging abstract imagery with clear type
__ Creating depth and texture within an image

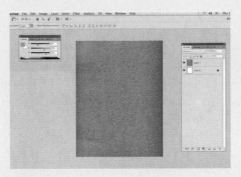

01____ As I want this piece to have a worn, retro feel to it, I find that using background images such as the one in the screen grab make a great starting point. Find a similar stock image or scan an image in yourself. I set the Opacity to 55%, the Fill to 18% and select Multiply.

02____ A great way to work with some really interesting colours is to experiment with the Swatches panel in the drop-down menu to the right of the Swatches column. For this piece I will be using a Pantone solid matte.

04____ Now we have the background in place, it's time to work on the illustration. I've chosen an image of an oil refinery as a focal point. I use the Pen tool to cut the image out accurately, and I also cut out other images, such as a car, to feature in the piece.

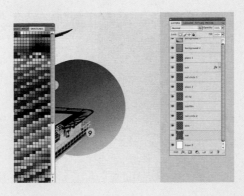

03____ For a spray paint effect, select a large round brush, around 1000px in size with Hardness at 0. Whilst holding Shift, click around the canvas. Once you have done this a few times, turn the Opacity down to around 24% and the Fill to about 35%.

05____ Once you have cut out your images, go to Image>Adjustments> Levels and Hue/Saturation to bring out the black and white more. Select a few other stock object images, cut them out, and go to Image>Adjustments>Photo Filter to add an aged effect to these.

06____ Next, to add some colourful shapes, use the Ellipse and Pen tools with the Shape Layers icon checked. Then add a gradient by going to Layer>Rasterize>Shape, selecting each shape with the Magic Wand tool and dragging the Gradient tool across.   →

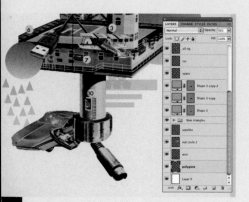

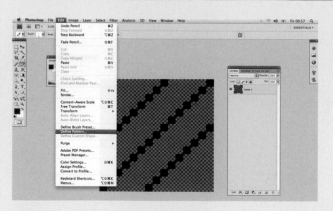

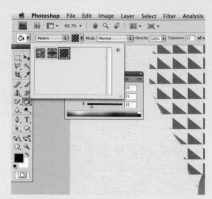

07_____ To create multiple shapes, use the Pen tool as in Step 6 to create, for instance, a triangle. Once that's created, hold Alt/Opt, move the cursor and it will copy the layer. Do this a number of times and group the layers by adding a new group.

08_____ Let's create some diagonal line patterns. Open a new image, 15x15px with a transparent background, and select the Pencil tool. Decide on the thickness of your pencil (and, therefore, your lines). For this example I am using 1pt. Go to Edit>Define Pattern. Using the Paint Bucket tool, you can now fill any shape with the pattern by selecting the Pattern button option.

09_____ Experiment even further by creating other patterns, such as the triangles shown. Using the same process as in Step 8, I've set my brush at 455 before creating some random shapes and filling them with the desired pattern using the Paint Bucket tool.

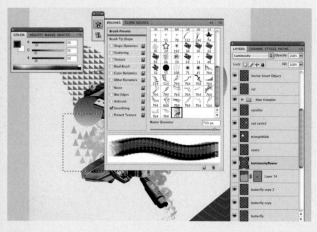

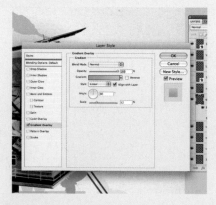

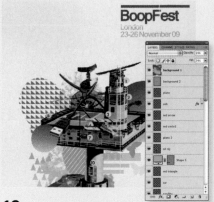

10_____ Open the brushes.psd file from the disc, marquee an image and go to Edit>Define Brush to make this an editable brush. I want the brushes to appear subtly in the background so, whilst holding down Shift and pressing + or -, I go through different blending modes and use the Luminosity option.

11_____ Now it's time to fire up Illustrator to add the text. File>Place your Photoshop illustration to use as a guideline for setting up your type. I decide to use a clear sans-serif font with 2pt weight for the title, and add bold lines to differentiate the type from the image.

12_____ Once happy with the type, delete the illustration, go to File>Export and save as Photoshop.psd. Back in Photoshop, open the type, line it up as it was in Illustrator and layer it above the background layers. You can place more objects from objects.psd, on the disc.

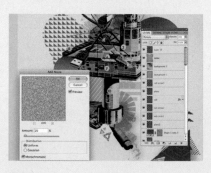

13_____ To add even more touches, I duplicate my 'Red Circle 2' layer, select Filter>Blur>Radial blur, choose the 'Spin' blur method, type 100 in the Amount box and select 'Best' quality. I do the same with an ink drop layer I have created, but this time go to Gaussian blur and set Amount to around 65. I set the new layers behind the originals.

14_____ You can spruce vector layers up even more by using the blending options available in Photoshop. I use a gradient overlay on one of the vector layers, duplicate the layer that has the USB cable image on it, and add a series of bold red lines across the illustration.

15_____ For the finishing touches, I want to make the whole image look a little rougher so I add a new layer and fill it with light grey. I then go to Filter> Noise>Add Noise, set it to around 20% and set it as Multiply. Finally, I rest this layer on top of the image.

CUSTOM BUILT BY ROCK FANS, FOR ROCK FANS

MAMA FESTIVALS
&
ROCK PRESENT

HIGH VOLTAGE
FESTIVAL

(24TH JULY 2010)   **(25TH JULY 2010)**

VINYL EXCHANGE, CLASSIC ROCK CINEMA
BEER TENT, CLASSIC MOTORBIKE & CAR EXHIBITION

SATURDAY + SUNDAY JULY 24/25, 2010
LONDON VICTORIA PARK

TICKETING INFO:
LIMITED EARLY BIRD JUMP THE QUEUE (EXPIRES DEC 31ST 2009)
DAY TICKET £65.00 (NO BOOKING FEE)
WEEKEND TICKET £120.00 (NO BOOKING FEE)

FESTIVAL'S 24 HOUR HOTLINE: 0871 230 5582
ONLINE BOOKINGS WWW.HIGHVOLTAGEFESTIVAL.COM
JAZZ CAFÉ BOX OFFICE, CAMDEN.
OPENING HOURS MONDAY TO SATURDAY 10.30AM TO 5.30PM

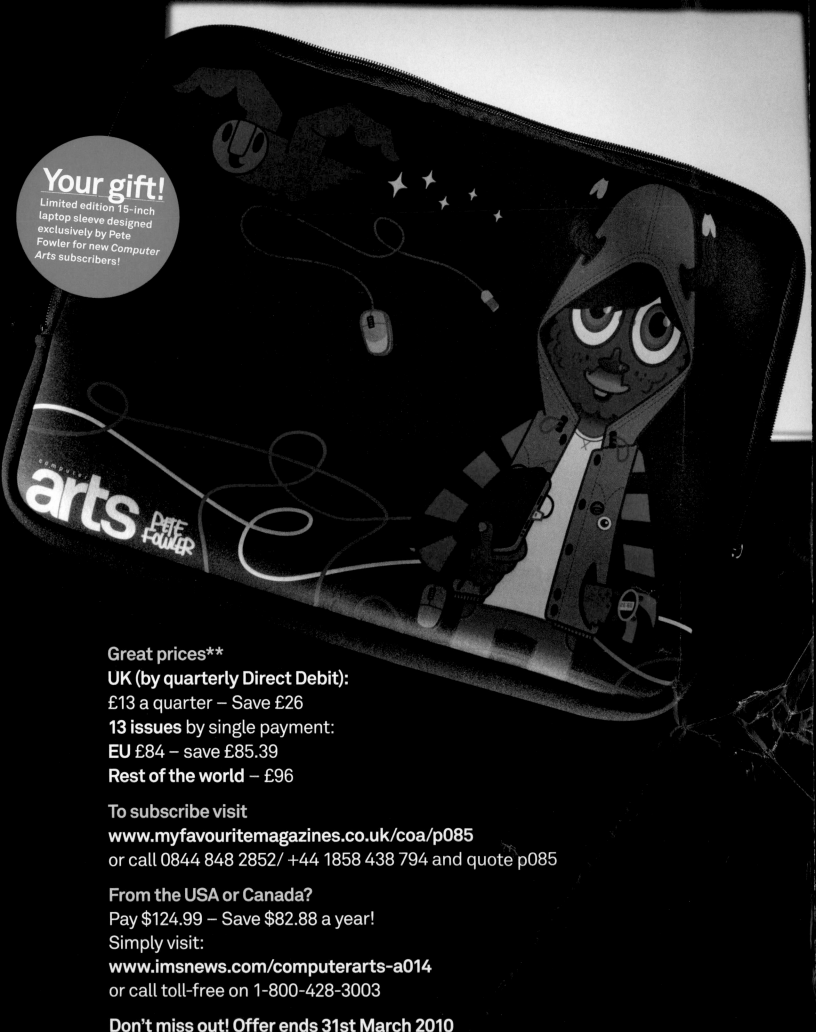

Exclusive international subscription offer!
Subscribe & save over £26* a year
PLUS get this exclusive laptop case designed by Pete Fowler

Pete Fowler, one of the UK's best-known character illustrators and the brains behind *Monsterism*, is famous for his cast of colourful characters. He's designed this limited-edition 15-inch laptop sleeve exclusively for new *Computer Arts* subscribers!

Benefits of subscribing to your favourite design mag
- Have every issue delivered direct to your home or workplace, wherever you are in the world
- Get this amazing gift and save up to £83 off the newsstand price!
- Never miss an issue
- Stay up to date with all the latest trends and industry news
- Get 13 issues a year!

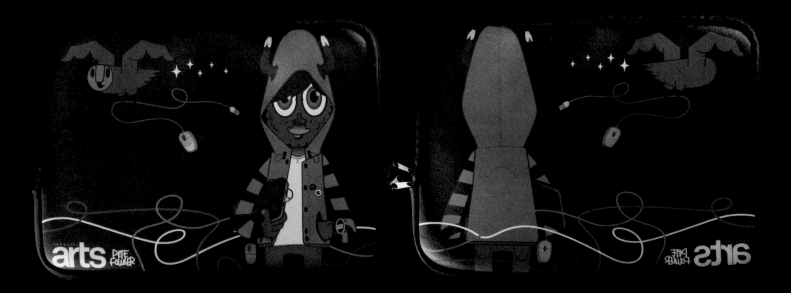

Need to Know

Keeping you up to date with the latest technology and industry developments

3D made easy
See below
Software tools abound to improve the pace and effects of your work in 3D. But are they right for you?

Font matches
Page 121
Jacob Cass introduces the 10 failsafe font combinations that signal an end to type selection traumas

Campaign council
Page 122
10 advertising and design experts reveal their methods for ensuring your cross-media campaign flies

G-Pen M712X
Page 124
Can the new tablet offering from Genius steal Wacom's graphics tablet crown? We assess the M712X

3D made easy

It takes talent to stand out on the page, and the best 3D tools can offer a helping hand. But are they right for you and your work?

The problem with 2D illustration is that it can look so... flat. Designers have been creating 2.5D effects almost since the first release of Illustrator and Photoshop. But for some 3D work, it can be hard to beat the real thing.

The challenge is finding the trade-off between time and productivity. Drawing 3D effects by hand is time consuming, but it's not necessarily any more of a time sink than rigging a 3D scene in a 3D modelling package. In fact, 3D software isn't essential, as Photoshop can be highly flexible.

"For 'Chocolate Dreams' I decided to go for a 3D atmosphere, because chocolate is so physical," designer Rik Oostenbroek explains. "This was a purely abstract project – no photos or references were used – in Photoshop only. I started with just a circle with a brown-black gradient. I always make my shapes with the Pen tool and drop a gradient in it. Whenever I make a shape with the Pen tool, I just make a path, to have more freedom with filling in the gradient. I like to play around and see what happens – for example, trying out almost an entire palette of colours to see which ones suit the chocolate brown the best."

Oostenbroek employs tried-and-tested techniques to achieve a 3D effect without specific 3D software. "The background is a simple gradient," continues the designer, "like every single shape in the piece – I modify these gradients into an atmospheric shape with a tablet. To fine-tune it, I use my soft brush in Photoshop to give it some light and shadow on the gradient. After two hours of brushing, shading and lightening, I could finally see a suggestion of the final result."

This is old school hands-on illustration, and it can produce impressive results. But there are limits to what's possible when it comes to three-dimensional effects. 3D software wins hands down when a scene has to be re-lit or re-rendered from a different angle. Once you have a scene, it's easy to rework it as long as your software is in the sweet spot between power and productivity. But this is a balance that much 3D software is still struggling to reach, as German illustrator Mark Gmehling explains: "I started learning modelling in →

01

01 Rik Oostenbroek
chooses his graphics tablet over 3D software to bring depth to works such as 'Abstract Heart'

01-02 Mark Gmehling's *Drinschseries* comprises colourful characters that owe their three-dimensional facade to Cinema 4D

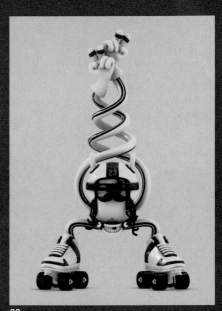

01

02

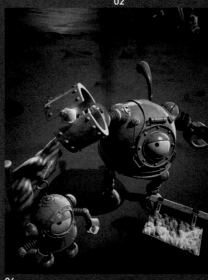

03-04 Gmehling takes many of his 3D illustrations through to **animation**. You can see his characters in action on www.markgmehling. weebly.com

03

04

Case study: 3D artist Mark Gmehling

Mark Gmehling began working with 3D in 1996, at first working with Bryce before moving on to Maya. But he soon found a more comfortable home with Maxon's Cinema 4D. "Cinema 4D release 6 looked simplest to me – things worked intuitively and it was obvious how to switch from Maya," Gmehling recalls. "So I've stayed with Cinema 4D, and I've been developing my skills as the program has grown. New releases seemed to fit with my development as a user. Today with v11.5 I see it on the same level as those old-school monster applications that used to rule the 3D market.

"My standard workflow is all about saving time and money. First the idea or brief are discussed with a client. After that I develop an idea with quick 2D scribbles, offering as many possibilities as I can and discussing every detail with the client. The 2D scribble becomes a coloured sketch that's signed off. Finally I create a 3D object – it's the very last part of the process, once I know what I'm trying to achieve. It's similar when I develop my personal projects, but I'm a difficult client, and the most important thing is to make decisions so that the project can be finished."

02 In this illustration for *Publish* magazine, **Rik Oostenbroek** makes clever use of shading to give the model's environment a surreal sense of depth

03 Rik Oostenbroek's 'Chocolate Dreams' was inspired by the physical forms that chocolate – both solid and liquid – can take

03

02

→ Maya, but the rendering and lighting possibilities were too much for me. The other big name package, 3ds Max, is still the dark side of the force to me – I hated the interface instantly. I see mindblowing stuff produced with 3ds Max, and I have a lot of respect for people who work with it, but I found learning to deal with that UI took all of the fun out of experimentation – and fun is the most important factor in 3D."

So for most illustrators, there's no need to master the high end; the famous-name packages are expensive, and difficult to use. Hollywood studios can afford to have different artists modelling, rigging, texturing, lighting and animating a scene, but that's a lot to take on if you're working on your own. The more budget-oriented packages may not pack in as many features, but you'll get more done in less time. And they cost less, too, with the added benefit that true 3D segues neatly into other professional creative services such as animation.

"The main fascination of 3D is that all components I love – audio and visual – come together in animation," says Gmehling. "It is like giving birth to something that comes out of your inner world, and I can wake it up, and make live and act. That moment is worth the time it takes [to create]. Next to that, the speed can be amazing – you can create something completely weird but realistic. There really are no borders."

3D power tools
Three of the finest 3D design aids

Adobe Photoshop CS4 Extended
Price: £950.29
URL: www.adobe.com
Photoshop CS3 included basic 3D effects, but CS4 Extended includes the ability to import, paint and texture 3D models. However, the selection of built-in lighting options is limited, so it's not a substitute for a full-featured 3D package. It's certainly good enough to get you started, though.

Maxon Cinema 4D
Price: £711.85
URL: www.maxon.net
A very popular mid-priced choice, C4D contains most of the rendering power of Maya and 3ds Max, but with a simpler interface. The one weakness is character animation. Otherwise, though, it's powerful, relatively easy to work with, and it renders compositing information for animations.

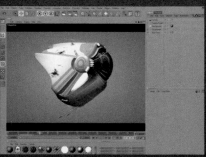

Strata Design 3D CX
Price: £435
URL: www.strata.com
With impressive photorealism and powerful CS integration via included plug-ins, Strata Design 3D offers a lot of power at a relatively low price. The full CX suite costs around twice as much, but includes a wider selection of tools, including Foto, which can turn photos into 3D objects.

10 failsafe font combinations

We take the pain out of font matching by selecting 10 combinations that will always work well together

Choosing a typeface for your design isn't always an easy task, and fixing on a successful pairing can be a particularly arduous task. One general rule of thumb when combining fonts is to use a serif and a sans serif together, to create contrast. Here we look at 10 great font combinations that never fail to fit; the way they have been combined is based on using two complementing typefaces – one for the heading and one for the body copy – with both being interchangeable. For this reason, we would recommend that you experiment with different sizes, weights, leading and so forth to get the most from your chosen typefaces.

1. Georgia & Verdana

For those who stick to web standards, this combination is always going to be a winner. By coupling the beautiful serif typeface that is Georgia with Verdana, a sans-serif font that was designed for the screen, you'll hit upon a match that will never fail.

2. Helvetica (Bold) & Garamond

This is a classic combination that will always please – who doesn't love a large headline set in Helvetica Bold? The clean and neutral nature of Helvetica makes it a perfect partner for Garamond, one of the most legible printed serif typefaces around.

3. Bodoni & Futura

Bodoni's geometric construction and blend of thick and thin strokes make it a true beauty of a font. Combined with Futura, it becomes part of a true power pairing – just ask any fashion magazine.

4. Franklin Gothic (Demi) & Baskerville

Baskerville is an old-style classic designed in 1757 which, when combined with the sans-serif 19th-century typeface Franklin Gothic, makes for an appealing contrast and gives your design that additional touch of sophistication. Try experimenting with the condensed versions of Franklin Gothic for a really attention-grabbing headline.

5. Caslon (Bold) & Univers (Light)

Caslon is a robust serif typeface that is characterised by short ascenders and descenders with a moderate modulation of stroke. It works extremely well with the rather neutral Univers, a neo-grotesque sans-serif typeface. When using Univers as your display font, try utilising the condensed weights.

6. Frutiger (Bold) & Minion

Frutiger is an extremely legible typeface, originally designed for directional signage systems in airports, which makes it perfect for headlines. The organic, clean nature of this sans-serif face makes it a great match for the very readable Minion, a beautiful typeface that is inspired by the classical fonts of the late Renaissance.

7. Minion (Bold) & Myriad

The Minion Pro family is a must for any designer's arsenal. With its many ligatures, small caps, old-style figures, swashes and other added glyphs, Minion Pro is ideal for a multitude of jobs. In combination with the versatility of Myriad, this is even more true – just ask Adobe.

8. Gill Sans (Bold) & Garamond

These fonts come installed by default on most operating systems, which makes this duo a good choice for those with even the most basic software set-up. Gill Sans is one of those fonts that will couple up nicely with just about any other, so it is extremely versatile. Originally designed for use on the London Underground, it is highly legible and, when combined with such classics as Garamond, it can work visual wonders.

9. Clarendon & Trade Gothic

The slab serif Clarendon attracts attention at large sizes and is also quite legible at smaller point sizes thanks to its clear, objective and timeless forms. It works particularly well when paired with the earthy naturalism of Trade Gothic. If using Trade Gothic as the headline face, make sure you check out the condensed weights.

10. Avenir & Minion

Although Avenir owes some of its interpretation to Futura ('avenir' translates as 'future' in French, after all), the typeface is not purely geometric; it has vertical strokes that are thicker than the horizontals, and shortened ascenders. This enables Avenir to work for both display and body copy, and to nestle very comfortably alongside old-style serif fonts such as Minion.

Cross-media campaign secrets

Anyone can run a cross-platform campaign, but engaging an audience with a single message is no easy task. The experts reveal their tricks for success

1

Understand the audience
Daniele Fiandaca
CEO (Europe), Profero
www.profero.com/uk
"The best cross-media campaigns have a really good and simple idea at their core, executed within the media which best suits the audience. Understand where the audience is and then make sure that you use the media appropriately to bring the idea to life. It is not about matching luggage."

2

Suit the message to the medium
Ben Clapp
Creative director, Spike
www.spikeuk.com
"The key to creative success is to understand, interpret and execute the idea appropriately in each category. Moving from offline to online may mean changing the tone of the piece to have more cut-through, or 'breaking the fourth wall', letting people interact with the work, get involved and share ownership."

3

Don't obsess with online
Hoss Gifford
Digital director, Marque
www.marquecreative.com
"It's important that each medium is given the freedom to stray from the campaign sufficiently to capitalise on it's own strengths. Five years ago, online campaigns were creatively limited by the primary medium – usually television or print. Now I fear online may be limiting the creative possibilities of offline mediums."

4

Play the fame game
Hugh Baillie
Chief executive,
Ogilvy Advertising
www.ogilvy.co.uk
"[Create] an asset that you can build your campaign around, which transfers across a lot of different media. So, in the old world, the orange man in Tango [ads] could be transferred around lots of places. The Cadbury's gorilla does that. It's simple, understandable and generates fame."

Think usefulness and context
Jon Bains
Founder, Lateral
www.lateral.net
"You want something that's multi-threaded, that's going to engage in lots of different ways, and ideally something that helps [the public] do something that they hadn't necessarily appreciated that they wanted or needed to do. [With] social media, it's about ideas that are genuinely behaviour-driven and have a social context."

Don't be isolated
Jens Bachem
MD, Digital Outlook
www.digital-outlook.com
"Genuine cross-media campaigns that really engage the audience are incredibly rare. Agencies tend to work in silos. In my view, we need a single audience-led, shared campaign objective – purchase intent, for argument's sake – with every media specialist heavily incentivised to deliver against it."

Single out a visionary
Kieron Leppard
Usability experience architect,
Fortune Cookie
www.fortunecookie.co.uk
"There needs to be someone at the front with a clear vision of what needs to be achieved. They're the person who's really going to champion the campaign, who really understands what you're trying to achieve as a group rather than as separate work streams."

Don't leash ideas to one post
Richard Neville
MD, Spike
www.spikeuk.com
"Make sure your idea is not tied to one particular platform (such as TV). We think the key is to have an idea capable of interaction. That doesn't mean it absolutely has to be digital. It just needs to be something that your audience feels it can get involved in."

Be inspired by the product
Tom Hume
MD, Future Platforms
www.futureplatforms.com
"It's about trying to blur the lines between campaign and product. If you look at the things that agencies like RGA are doing, things like Nokia viNe or Nike+, it's more about producing a service that emphasises a brand's values than it is creating an ad campaign and microsite."

Be imaginative about physical space
Ross Taylor
Chief digital officer, TMW
www.tmw.co.uk
"Digital doesn't mean simply doing what you used to do [in a space] but quicker. You can change the entire way in which you think about that space, how you tie it into your mobile strategy, your social strategy, link to your advertising and use it more effectively than before."

Genius G-Pen M712X

Can Genius's G-Pen M712X tablet topple Wacom's dominance? We take a look

Genius's latest range of graphics tablets is markedly different from its traditional offerings, boasting a spec list usually associated with a high-end Wacom, but at a very consumer-friendly price.

The G-Pen M712X runs at 4,000LPI resolution, has a widescreen working area of 30.5x18.5cm and can be rotated from landscape to portrait while you work. It also combines 1024 levels of pressure sensitivity with a new pen and nib combination for super-precise sketching, while 34 assignable hot keys, zoom control and scroll wheel round things off nicely.

It might cost half the price of a top-spec Wacom, but the Genius G-Pen M712X is no slouch. It lacks the multi-touch properties of the Wacom Bamboo, and the multi-nib and pen offerings of an Intuos, but the M712X is more than capable of professional work.

Selectors
Two rotation selectors offer zoom, pan and rotate controls, and can also be assigned to resize brushes.

Hot keys
34 hot keys grace the inner edge of the tablet, all of which are assignable to prompt shortcuts and tool selections, and run macro features.

Surface
The M712X's 30.5x18.5cm surface area boasts 4,000LPI resolution and 1024 levels of pressure sensitivity.

Pen
While the pen may be battery powered (as opposed to Wacom's electro magnetic offering) it remains light, easy to use and packs two assignable buttons.

Genius G-Pen M712X
Price £87.95
URL: www.genius
tablet.com

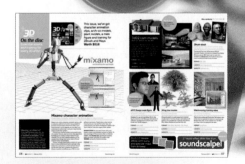

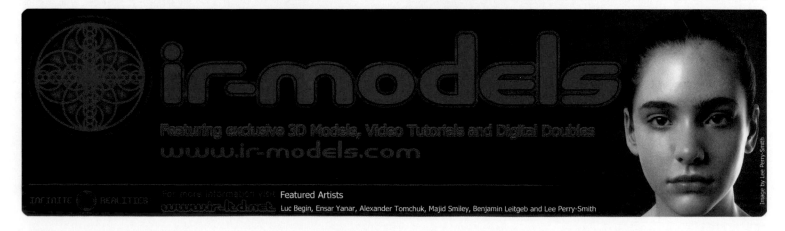

Mustard

The best new jobs.

Hello@wearemustard.com

55-80k
Art director
Above-the-line

Strategic individual with big ideas and a visual obsession sought by multi award winning agency. Email your five best examples of what you do best.

Creative director
Brand identity

Strategic brand positioning, identity and engagement consultancy seeks director. Consumer and financial brand exprience needed for rare opportunity.

Design director
FMCG/luxury packaging

Packaging opportunity for an up and coming star. Previous big agency experience essential for this great role. Suit designer with a pocket of awards.

30-50k
Senior
Branding designer

Uber-cool designer sought to work on stylish high street brand engagement. Big name brands. Visually stimulating: identity, guidelines, print, advertising.

Senior
Brand experience

Clerkenwell agency seeks typographical refinement, sophisticated branding designer to work on uber-cool brands Love crafted print. Love environments.

Senior
Spirits/alcohol packaging

Premium alcohol and spirits designer for award winning consultancy. Stylish, modern typographical detail obsessed individual needed. Fantastic new job.

28-32k
Middleweight
FMCG Packaging

Looking to move? New year, new job? Brand savy and ready to work on FMCG brands that compliment both your modern eye, big ideas and experience.

Middleweight
Spirits/alcohol packaging

Due to recent international pitch wins on big branded projects. Fun agency now seeks a premium alcohol/spirits star to join their winning team. Central London.

Freelance
Contract work

High street retail branding (3 months), Packaging FMCG (5 months), Spirit /alcohol packaging middleweight. Cigarette packaging middleweight.

Exposure

Send us your images and get your work seen by a worldwide audience of creative professionals

How to get exposed
Send your work to us on CD or DVD, along with details of your location, job title, techniques and software, the title of each piece, your website and email address. Wherever possible, illustrations should be sent as high-resolution AI files, TIFFs or JPEGs. If possible, please include a hard copy. We will endeavour to return all entries that include a self-addressed envelope.

All contributions are submitted to us on the basis of a non-exclusive worldwide licence to publish, both in print and electronically.

Post high-resolution files for print to:
Exposure, *Computer Arts*, 30 Monmouth Street, Bath, BA1 2BW, United Kingdom

Helen Mycroft
Location Sydney, Australia
Job Illustrator/graphic designer
Contact www.helenmycroft.co.uk
Software Illustrator, Photoshop

Having graduated from the University of Lincoln last year, Helen Mycroft is currently living in Australia while looking for work placements and creating artwork before her return to the UK.

"All my works starts on paper, but I can usually visualise how I want the final image to look from the moment I start," she says, "so I have a very clear idea of the direction and process,"

She especially enjoys looking in unusual places to find inspiration – and has plenty of it: "My parents had a lot of their childhood things given away so they resolved to never do the same thing to me and my sisters, so now I have this massive collection of rare things that I can used for inspiration."

01 Life Isn't Fair
"This is one of my dad's favourite sayings," laughs Mycroft, "and after hearing him say it so many times when I'm having a whinge, I made it into a poster. It was designed in Illustrator from a mix of typefaces, with the shading added in Photoshop."

02 Gone Too Far
The cover artwork for a journal Mycroft made, containing a selection of visual references and photos from her "adventures" in both the UK and Australia. "There have been two issues so far," she explains, "and they're great to flick through when I'm stuck for ideas."

01

02

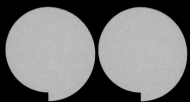 **I love creating my own character shapes and seeing what I can do in terms of creating visuals from them**

Chris Osment
Location Somerset, UK
Job Illustrator/designer
Contact www.killstudio.co.uk
Software Illustrator, Photoshop, InDesign

"With so much inspiration floating about in our world, I find it difficult not to get excited by new concepts and ideas," says Chris Osment. He now channels those ideas through Killstudio, the business he set up in February of last year, having previously graduated from The Arts Institute in Bournemouth in 2005 and then worked for a studio in the south-west of England.

"I was always taught from early on in my creative years that I should try to absorb everything around me and use it to my advantage through my creativity," Osment adds. This has manifested through work for clients such as Volkswagen and Penguin in Killstudio's short life to date, and the designer has plans to expand further, launching an online shop very soon. "I can honestly say I love my job and the industry I'm in!" he says.

03 Typo Experimento
A personal piece and typography experiment. "I've always been interested in shapes and form, especially within typography," says Osment. "I love creating my own character shapes and seeing what I can do in terms of creating visuals from them. This promotional piece just concentrates on form and simplicity, allowing the letter shapes to work with each other inside a closed space."

04 Shameless Licks
Created for the UK band Shameless Licks, this poster for their debut EP *Lick It Up* fits inside the EP packaging. "It has a very 'galactic' feel to it," says Osment, "almost as if you're looking through the words into another world. The inspiration came from thoughts of empty space – free-flowing movement inside a solid structure."

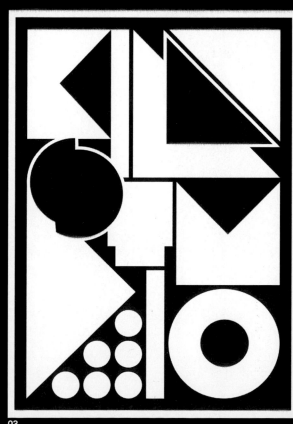

03

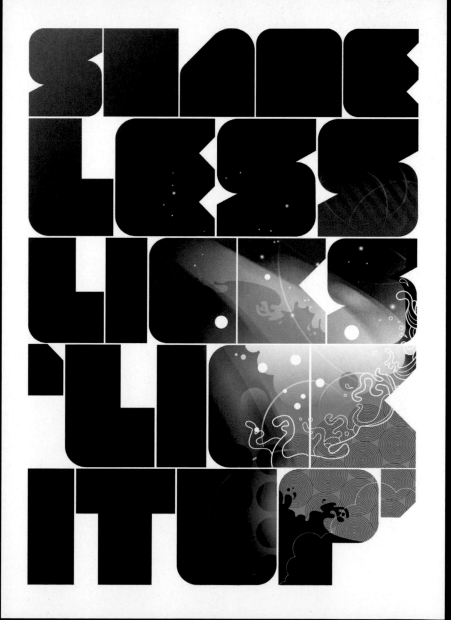

04

Jon Haste
Location London
Job Illustrator
Contact www.kolbillustration.com
Software Photoshop, Illustrator

I always work within a narrative, with the image representing a piece of a story

Despite completing a degree in 3D Design, Jon Haste – aka KOLB – soon found that he much preferred 2D work. Once he'd landed a job as an in-house illustrator at a Brazilian newspaper, he began gradually building up his illustration portfolio.

"KOLB, my studio, was initially created as a showcase for that illustrative work, setting itself apart from the more graphic design-orientated work I've produced," Haste explains. "I always work within a narrative, with the image representing a piece of a story or text, or an imagined event. It's the illustration of the moment that inspires the work, and I bring as much feeling and emotion to it as I can muster."

05 Face of a Thousand Fists
"I'd had an idea of creating an image with hands or body parts, a concept that isn't new," Haste explains, "but I wanted to add extra dimensions in detail, almost so that the hands or body parts are unrecognisable and take on a different quality in the image. It came about quite quickly once this idea had materialised."

06 The Orchard is Such a Very Silly Place
"This four-colour screenprint sprang out from some sketches I was making while playing around with positive and negative shapes," says Haste of this illustration. "The environment and storylines playing out within the wood are oblivious to the mischievous creatures all around them."

05

06

Heinritzh Sales
Location Manila, Philippines
Job Graphic designer
Contact www.ritzh.carbonmade.com
Software Photoshop

Heinritzh Sales is another artist who changed his mind regarding his career. After graduating from an engineering course, he took the decision to become a graphic designer instead, armed with little more than a few T-shirt design contest successes and some friends in the creative industry. Eventually – "with guts and Photoshop to back me up," he says – Sales applied for his first design job at leading Philippines clothing label Folded and Hung.

"It's really a dream come true, seeing your designs on the streets worn by different people whom you don't even know," Sales enthuses. More recently he has joined another well-regarded local studio, Team Manila, and seems to have found his niche.

"Designing for me is not a 9-to-5 job," he continues. "It hunts me any time and anywhere – while riding on a bus, taking a shower or even while I'm sleeping. Ideas will come naturally in the least expected situation. Just remember that when that moment comes, don't store it in your brain; write it down so you can free up some kilobytes of memory in your head."

07 Random Thoughts
One of Sales' T-shirt designs, which is currently featured on clothing from The Inksquad. "I chose a bird silhouette symbolising freedom," says the designer. "I think it just fits well with the randomness of the thoughts written on it. Doing something like this is total freedom for me. I just write what I want, and what I feel."

08 Pleasure
Another T-shirt design, mixing typography, hand-made type, drawings and symbols. Sales says he chose the silhouette of a woman because of its "sophisticated, fragile and yet dangerous characteristics... well actually, it's just a good shape to start with. There are no fancy meanings behind it. I chose words at random again – and it takes a lot of patience because it consumes hours for such a project, from start to finish."

> **Doing something like this is total freedom for me. I just write what I feel**

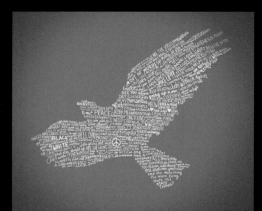

Oriol Fernandez Tur
Location Barcelona, Spain
Job Graphic designer
Contact www.urikane.com
Software Photoshop

As I don't normally find the right words, I try to find the right images

"Since I was a child I've had a problem with language," says Oriol Fernandez Tur. "I'm dyslexic and I think it helps me to see words as objects, not just as words. I like experimenting with them and playing on the limits of comprehension."

Unsurprisingly, then, much of Tur's work incorporates typography in some form, although often meanings (and double-meanings) are twisted and played on in an interesting manner. "I don't have a strict way of working," he explains. "Sometimes I start with a pencil, and sometimes I go straight to the computer. I like experimenting with each project, but most of the time I prefer starting with a concept." In fact, Tur's difficulty with words seems to have been of some benefit to his art, at least: "As I don't normally find the right words, I try to find the right images."

09 Anatomie
Tur was inspired by scientific illustrations in school textbooks for this piece: "I like the idea of drawing something and explaining its different parts, creating a story with all this information. I chose a man who has birds living on him because I like the idea of isolation. He is like an ecosystem." The text is prominent – and in French. "I don't really speak French," Tur continues, "but I wanted to judge the illustration for its colours, typography, shapes and so on, not its message."

10 Vine a ca la Meri
The title of this piece, which was essentially a poster invite for a party, translates as 'Come to Meri's House'. While working on the image, Tur decided that the best way to read the text was from front to back. "Then I saw I was wrong, because everyone reads 'Meri la a ca Vine'… anyway, the party was packed, so I concluded that people get smart when a party is on." He adds that he has always liked 3D typography: "I enjoy the contrast you get when you combine a drawn technique with 'real' perspective."

09

10

TakeCare
Location Moscow
Job Graphic designer
Contact www.thelocalgenius.com
Software Photoshop

"Someone who can really teach must be learning himself, and people who enjoy teaching others usually have too much free time and too little wisdom," says TakeCare – AKA Kostya Sasquatch from Russia – rather controversially. It's hardly a surprise though, as he adds that he finds classic art and the academic style of teaching boring. "I consider life itself to be the serious study, where you can't practise in one discipline above all others."

One of the things that had the strongest impact on him, Sasquatch says, was broadband internet, "enabling me to watch thousands of images, videos and other art from all over the world. In 2005 my future bride Lisa and I created our first website with our own art... Although it doesn't seem that long ago, I wonder how much I've learnt within those five years. I hope this evolution never stops."

11 Donut Control
"The donut is a symbol of eternity in the 3D evolution of the circle," says TakeCare, perhaps not entirely seriously. "It also has taken its place in science-related culture after the remarkable topological example of the similarity of a donut (torus) and a mug." One of a series of images which TakeCare claims to not even understand himself, he adds that "the style is clear, with simple shapes and some special and considered details."

12 Bottom
"This is just about the beauty of a woman's body. In spite of a definite erotic context, the mood of the image is very calm and tender, but still sensual because of very soft, smooth shapes, with almost no contrast. All the details have very exact proportions. I've also made few colourful versions, but this I consider to be the best of them."

> I wonder how much I've learnt in five years. I hope this evolution never stops

WE CONTROL
THE DONUTS

11

12

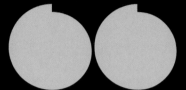

I'm comfortable creating storytelling work that has a strong connection to fantasy ⬤⬤

Nina Hunter
Location Leeds, UK
Job Graphic designer
Contact www.ninahunter.com
Software Photoshop, Illustrator

"During my career I have developed a unique feminine style in graphic design and illustration," says Nina Hunter, "which led to me to leaving my full-time job and setting up a creative agency called LoveLife, focusing on the female market and the fashion and beauty industry." LoveLife, she adds, is designed to showcase female design in an industry seemingly dominated by men.

Originally from Gdansk in Poland, where she graduated with an MA in Fine Arts, Hunter now lives and works in the UK. She combines the development of LoveLife with her own career. "I've recently been exploring the art of digital illustration; the digital collage, a relatively new art form, is a combination of a skilled hand and modern technology."

13 Alice in Wonderland
Hunter began working on this series of images a few months ago. "My illustrations are not truthful representations of the story, they are just inspired by it," she says. "I find myself very comfortable creating storytelling work that has a very strong connection to fantasy. In this illustration I have used elements of Polish folk art to add a bit of identity and make reference to my home country." Several of the images have appeared at the Gallery North exhibition in Batley, and she also hopes to collaborate with a fashion designer to print some of this work onto clothing.

14 Time
An earlier work that has also appeared in exhibitions. "The illustration is supposed to graphically present the importance of our existence and of time — it being our most precious commodity and crucial aspect of our existence," says Hunter. "The symbolic time of five-minutes-to-midnight doesn't seem to bother the beautiful girl, who is sitting relaxed and unaware of what's happening. Meanwhile, the time is running out and the clock is falling apart, disappearing forever. It's a philosophical illustration that makes us stop and contemplate the aim of the race we're all part of."

13

14

Next Issue

computer
arts

Issue 172 on sale Thursday 11 February

Software skills
Motion graphics in
After Effects
Master Flash's Morph
and Warp tools
Plus much more!

Illustration to animation
New techniques to make your still images move!

Mario Hugo
We catch up with the design icon in his New York studio

Photograph Reynard Li

01-02 Physalia's experimental labour of love, *Timelapsus*

03-04 Intricate artist-illustrator **Rob Hunt's** retro chaos landscapes

computer

arts

○ Disc
_171

Taking the time to improvise

How many times have you dreamt up a cunning design concept, then looked at the tools at your disposal and felt the task to be impossible? At this point, some give up. Others, however, choose to improvise. And that's just what Spanish outfit Physalia did in the creation of their experimental short *Timelapsus*.

The three-man team set about building a motion control robotic rig, and even designed its software in order to film the piece using a digital reflex photo camera. They then took the real-time day-to-night time-lapse photo sequence and painstakingly mixed in aquatic 3D animation.

The whole process took five months, yet it proves that, with a little vision and ingenuity, you don't have to be James Cameron and have a million-dollar budget to realise your design dreams.

01

02

03

04

Output

Alex Guimerá
Showreel from the Spanish designer with a passion for viewing life through a lens

Challenge Your World
Stunning short from Julien Nantiec

Dove Nets
Ben&Julia produce animation magic for the band The Main Drag

Earl Cabuhat
Impressive showreel from a Canadian name to watch

James Kearsley
Reel showing the astounding 3D, CGI and photorealism work from JK Studios

Rod Hunt
Wonderfully observed characters in a retro setting

Segura Inc
Brilliant work from our Open Studios feature subject

Timelapsus
VFX and motion design studio Physalia Studios' experimental short

;phunk studio
Portfolio picks from another Open Studios feature star

Acrobat 9 Pro video training
Total Training gives you the Acrobat 9 Pro essentials

30 free fonts
A collection of typefaces for you to use in your designs

Modern Dog clip art
Modern Dog provides a taste of its diverse series of clip art collections

Acrobat tutorial
How Acrobat 9 Pro can help you get interactive

Get Flash in Illustrator
Work seamlessly between Illustrator and Flash

Explosive motion graphics
The first in our two-part tutorial on animating a graphic sequence

Webcam photo mosaics
Build photo mosaic masterpieces with your webcam and Flash

Cross-platform characters
Give your character designs multi-platform versatility

Links

All the Computer Arts links you need

01 JK Studios' effects-laden showreel positively sparkles

02 See more of Chicago-based design firm **Segura Inc** in this issue's Open Studios feature

computer
arts
o Disc
_171

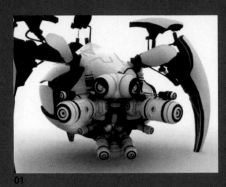
01

02

February 2010
Highlights

Dove Nets
The Main Drag music video from Ben&Julia

Timelapsus
Experimental short from Physalia Studio

Challenge Your World
Julien Nantiec's awesome short

Acrobat 9 Pro video training
Total Training unveils the Acrobat Pro 9 essentials

Free fonts
30 free fonts for you to incorporate into your designs

Tutorial files
Everything you need to complete this month's Technique tutorials

computer
arts
Disc
_171

Computer Arts is a registered trademark of Future Publishing Ltd

future

© Future PLC 2009
CA171 CD February 2010
Made in the EU

Using the CD
The CD should auto-run when you insert it into your CD drive. If not, run either CA.exe for Windows or Arts for the Mac. To toggle auto-run on and off, use the Control Panel on your computer. You'll need a web browser and an active internet connection. If you have problems using this disc, please email ca.support@futurenet.co.uk.

This is a Future Computing CD-ROM
This disc has been thoroughly scanned and tested at all stages of production, but – as with all new software – we still recommend you run a virus checker before use. We also recommend you have an up-to-date backup of your hard drive at all times. Although every effort is made to keep this CD virus-free, Future Publishing Ltd cannot accept responsibility for any disruption, damage and/or loss to your data or computer system that may occur while using this CD and this programs and data on it.

Any comments?
Send your comments and suggestions for improvements to Computer Arts' new media editor at ca.mail@futurenet.co.uk, or by post at Computer Arts, Future Publishing, 30 Monmouth Street, Bath BA1 2BW.

For technical support, you can contact us using one of the following:
1_ The web – www.futurenet.co.uk/support.
Here you'll find details of previously solved problems, updates and patches.
2_ Email – ca.support@futurenet.co.uk.
3_ Fax – 01225 732279.
4_ Telephone – call 01225 442244 on weekdays between 10am and 6pm and be sure to ask for a device's support.

Defective CDs
If your CD has signs of physical damage or you can't get the software to load because of read errors, contact our reader support team (phone – 01225 442244, email – ca.support@futurenet.co.uk). If the CD is faulty, we will send you a working version within 28 days.

future
MEDIA WITH PASSION